Dostoevsky's
Crime and Punishment

A Reader's Guide

Cultural Syllabus

Series Editor
Mark Lipovetsky (Columbia University)

Dostoevsky's
Crime and Punishment

A Reader's Guide

Deborah A. Martinsen

BOSTON
2022

Studies of the Harriman Institute

The Institute sponsors Studies of the Harriman Institute in the belief that their publication contributes to scholarly research and public understanding. In this way the Institute, while not necessarily endorsing their conclusions, is pleased to make available the results of some of the research conducted under its auspices.

Library of Congress Cataloging-in-Publication Data

Names: Martinsen, Deborah A., author.
Title: Dostoevsky's Crime and punishment : a reader's guide / Deborah
  Martinsen.
Description: Boston : Academic Studies Press, 2022. | Series: Cultural
  syllabus | Includes bibliographical references.
Identifiers: LCCN 2021055818 (print) | LCCN 2021055819 (ebook) | ISBN
  9781644697832 (hardback) | ISBN 9781644697849 (paperback) | ISBN
  9781644697856 (adobe pdf) | ISBN 9781644697863 (epub)
Subjects: LCSH: Dostoyevsky, Fyodor, 1821-1881. Prestuplenie i nakazanie. |
  Dostoyevsky, Fyodor, 1821-1881--Criticism and interpretation. | Russian
  literature--19th century--History and criticism.
Classification: LCC PG3325.P73 M37 2022 (print) | LCC PG3325.P73 (ebook)
  | DDC 891.73/3--dc23/eng/20211208
LC record available at https://lccn.loc.gov/2021055818
LC ebook record available at https://lccn.loc.gov/2021055819

ISBN 9781644697832 (hardback)
ISBN 9781644697849 (paperback)
ISBN 9781644697856 (adobe pdf)
ISBN 9781644697863 (epub)

Book design by PHi Business Solutions
Cover design by Ivan Grave. Artwork by Natalia Grave

Published by Academic Studies Press
1577 Beacon Street
Brookline, MA 02446, USA
press@academicstudiespress.com
www.academicstudiespress.com

With great gratitude for their patience and support,
I dedicate this book to my husband Randall Butler and our son Rory Butler.

Contents

Acknowledgments

This book was born in 1998 as a lecture for the faculty of Literature Humanities on how to teach *Crime and Punishment*. Over the years, as I taught Lit Hum and was invited to give further talks, I honed my strategy. The book in your hands (or on your screen) is thus the work of decades of thought. Many thanks go to my many readers, especially Nancy Workman, Amy Ronner, Caryl Emerson, Marcia Morris, Elizabeth Beaujour, Margo Shohl, Greta Matzner-Gore, Karin Beck, Maude Meisel, Gina Kovarsky, Jeffrie Murphy, and Sam Tecotzky. For guidance on narrative strategy, I am indebted to Robert L. Belknap, Robin Feuer Miller, Peter Rabinowitz, and Gary Rosenshield. For inviting me to give talks or suggest other *Crime and Punishment* speakers, I want to thank the many excellent Lit Hum Chairs, whom I have taught under—Robert L. Belknap, Kathy Eden, Cathy Popkin, Gareth Williams, Christia Mercer, Julie Crawford, and Joanna Stalnaker. Thanks also go to Katia Bowers and Kate Holland, who invited me to participate in a lively and memorable conference celebrating *Crime and Punishment* at 150. For their constant encouragement and friendship, I thank Carol Apollonio and Irina Reyfman. Further thanks go to all my students and interlocutors, named and unnamed, whose insights and enthusiasm have improved this project over the years.

I am grateful to Columbia College for giving me some of the time necessary to complete this project. I also thank the Harriman Institute for its institutional support. Special thanks go to Ron Meyer for his invaluable assistance during the last stages of manuscript preparation and for interfacing with the publisher. Thanks to Kirsten Painter for her thoughtful editing. Thanks also to the staff at Academic Studies Press, particularly Kate Yanduganova, for backing the project. I am particularly grateful to the Dostoevsky House-Museum in St. Petersburg, its director Natalia Ashimbaeva for facilitating the process of cover choice and permissions, and its associate director Boris Tikhomirov for providing illustrations and answering numerous queries.

Finally, I want to thank my family—my son Rory Butler for his patience and support and my husband Randall Butler for his steadfast encouragement, perspicacious editorial help, and unconditional love.

Introduction

Crime and Punishment is a psychological detective novel whose mystery lies not in the *whodunit* but in the *whydunit*—a question that perplexes protagonist and readers alike. The central character is a young man, who has succumbed to "certain strange 'unfinished' ideas floating in the air" (September 1865, letter to Katkov, 28/2:136).[1] His last name—Raskolnikov—signifies "schism" and marks him as a modern, divided self. He belongs to a generation of young people coming of age in a rapidly expanding media environment, where social justice issues such as extreme income inequality, court reforms, and the plight of women and children were discussed obsessively. Like other aspiring students-turned-journalists, Raskolnikov is seeking his own "new word." The discussion of his article "On Crime" shows that, like other reformers of his time, Raskolnikov is attracted to nihilism—a term designating an ideological amalgam of atheism, materialism, utilitarianism, feminism, and scientism that challenged existing beliefs, norms, and social institutions. After committing two murders—one ideological, one accidental—his punishment begins. As Dostoevsky wrote to Mikhail Katkov, the editor of *Russian Herald*, "Unresolved questions confront the murderer, unforeseen and unexpected feelings torment his heart" (September 1865, letter to Katkov, 28/2:136). Suffering from both intellectual doubts and feelings of alienation, he vacillates between the desires to confess and to escape.

This study of *Crime and Punishment* offers a reading of the novel that considers narrative strategy, psychology, and ideology. While written for the general reader of all levels, it also provides some suggestions for teaching. The focus on narrative strategy demonstrates how Dostoevsky first plunges readers into Raskolnikov's fevered brain, creating reader sympathy for him and explaining

---

1 All citations from Dostoevsky's works come from Fedor Mikhailovich Dostoevskii, *Polnoe sobranie sochinenii v tridtsati tomakh*, 30 vols. (Leningrad: Nauka, 1972–90). Because there are so many excellent translations of the novel, citations are noted by part and chapter (for example, part 1, chapter 2). Citations from his correspondence are noted by date, volume, and page number from the collected works (ex.: 28/2:136). All translations are mine, except when noted otherwise.

why most readers root for him to get away from the scene of the crime. By subsequently providing outsider perspectives on Raskolnikov's thinking, Dostoevsky effects a conversion in reader sympathy. The focus on psychology encourages readers to consider the difference between Raskolnikov's unconscious dreams (*sny*) and his conscious daydreams (*mechty*), thereby showing the deep conflict between his heart and his intellect. By examining the multiple justifications for murder Raskolnikov gives as he confesses to Sonya, this study highlights ideology and the novel's debunking of rationality-based theories. Finally, by considering the question of why Raskolnikov and most of the novel's male characters focus on the deliberate murder of the pawnbroker and forget the unintended murder of her half-sister Lizaveta, this study reveals a narrative strategy that focuses on shame and guilt. Because Raskolnikov has committed murder, readers expect him to feel guilt, which follows a defined script—remorse, repentance, expiation. Yet the novel portrays a man suffering from shame because he is not the extraordinary man he hoped to be. The novel thus keeps readers off-balance until the last pages of the Epilogue when it finally offers the guilt script and the resolution readers have been expecting all along.

While set in 1860s Russia, Dostoevsky's novel tackles many issues that resonate with contemporary audiences, including the alienation of modern man and the perils of ideology. *Crime and Punishment* demonstrates how individuals who are isolated tend to live inside their own heads, making them particularly vulnerable to the dangers of radical ideology. By espousing radical ideologies with absolute certainty, their adherents divide people. Moreover, such ideologies can blind us to facts and consequences, thereby blunting our essential human capacity to choose good over evil. The novel finally demonstrates both that love can close the gap between alienated individuals and that everyone is connected—concepts that may reverberate with today's internet-connected readers. Ultimately, as *Crime and Punishment* polemicizes with radical ideologies, it illustrates what can happen when ideas "floating in the air" lead an individual to commit and justify murderous acts—an issue as alive in today's world as it was in 1860s Russia. This study shows how ideology that promotes egoism can lead to crime, self-destruction, and misery. The study's five chapters thereby explain the enduring power of Dostoevsky's great novel.

CHAPTER 1

Historical Introduction: Dostoevsky and Russia

Fyodor Mikhailovich Dostoevsky's eventful life reflected his times. Born in Moscow in 1821 shortly before the reign of Nicholas I (1825–55), Dostoevsky died in Petersburg in 1881, six weeks before Alexander II was assassinated. Under Nicholas I, whose repressive regime controlled political thought and crushed dissent with restrictive policies on all facets of life, Dostoevsky was arrested, incarcerated, and exiled to Siberia. Under Alexander II, whose more liberal government initiated the Great Reforms needed to modernize Russia, Dostoevsky was allowed to return to Petersburg, participate in the era's lively journalistic debates, and write the novels that made him famous.

The second son of seven children, Fyodor Dostoevsky was raised on the grounds of the Mariinsky Hospital for the Poor, where his father, a former army surgeon, worked as a doctor. After his mother died when he was sixteen, Fyodor's father sent him and his older brother Mikhail to St. Petersburg, where Fyodor attended the St. Petersburg Academy of Engineers. There he excelled at drawing and spent much time reading. Although of medium size, Dostoevsky did his best to protect younger classmates from hazing.[1] He graduated in 1843 as a lieutenant, served briefly as a military engineer, and quickly resigned his commission to devote himself to writing.

After Dostoevsky finished writing his epistolary novella *Poor Folk* in the spring of 1845, he gained overnight fame and enjoyed a brief season of celebrity. Yet when his novella *The Double* was published in January 1846,

---

1   Joseph Frank, *Dostoevsky: The Seeds of Revolt, 1821–1849*, vol. 1 of *Dostoevsky*, 5 vols. (Princeton, NJ: Princeton University Press, 1976), 78.

Dostoevsky was criticized for his wordiness. In 1847, he met the utopian socialist Mikhail Butashevich-Petrashevsky and joined his circle. In 1848, as revolutions erupted throughout Europe, Dostoevsky joined a secret society within the Petrashevsky circle led by the charismatic Nikolai Speshnev. In 1849, Dostoevsky was arrested for reading a banned letter at a Petrashevsky circle meeting, incarcerated in the Peter-Paul military fortress for nine months, and condemned to death by firing squad. Awaiting execution in Semenovsky Square, Dostoevsky, shrouded, stood with the second group of three scheduled for death. He turned to his companion Speshnev and said, "*Nous serons avec le Christ*" (We'll be with Christ). To which Speshnev replied, "We shall be dust." A moment later, following Nicholas I's script, a drumroll resounded, and the firing squad lowered their rifles, ending the sadistic mock execution and inspiring the end-of-life motif that runs through much of Dostoevsky's subsequent writing.

Dostoevsky's sentence was commuted to four years of hard labor (1850–54) and exile in Siberia. As a political convict, he lived and worked in leg-irons in a Siberian prison, sharing close quarters with a multiethnic, largely illiterate group of peasant criminals from all reaches of the Russian empire. Dostoevsky was shocked by the cruelty of corporal punishment and the social divide between the educated and the peasants, who considered men like him part of the oppressing class. On top of the crowding and stench, Dostoevsky suffered intellectual privation: he had constant access to only one book—the New Testament.[2] Once released, he served five years as a military engineer in Omsk, where he married the widow Maria Isaeva. Although first diagnosed and treated in the 1840s for epilepsy, an illness that figures in both *The Idiot* and *The Brothers Karamazov*, Dostoevsky petitioned to return to Petersburg by claiming his seizures began during his incarceration.

In 1859, Dostoevsky returned to St. Petersburg and resumed his literary career. Arriving just before the serfs were liberated, he witnessed the end of the social evil that had prompted him to join the Petrashevsky circle and its radical wing. For the rest of his life Dostoevsky sympathized with radicals' aspirations for social harmony, but saw revolutionaries as truth-seekers and self-sacrificers gone astray. Post-Siberia, he wrote novels criticizing the ideas that drove revolutionaries' actions—*Crime and Punishment* is one of these. In this era of reform, Dostoevsky could travel extensively abroad, enjoy relaxed censorship, and,

---

2   In his memoirs, Petr Martyanov notes that Dostoevsky had occasional access to Dickens's *David Copperfield* and *The Pickwick Papers* while he was in the prison hospital.

most importantly, participate in the exciting public debates raging in Russia's proliferating print media.

Fyodor and his brother Mikhail eagerly joined the fray, launching two journals: *Time* (1861–63) and *Epoch* (1864–65). Although Dostoevsky's name was not displayed on the masthead because he was a former political prisoner, he served as the managing editor for both. He also provided editorials, ideological direction, and major works of fiction for them (including his semi-autobiographical novel *Notes from the House of the Dead* in 1861 and *Notes from Underground* in 1864). The 1864 deaths of Dostoevsky's first wife Maria and his brother Mikhail left Dostoevsky struggling to carry on the new journal *Epoch*, which closed in March 1865. Burdened by the journal's debts, as well as the care of his brother's family and his wife's son, Dostoevsky went on an unsuccessful gambling spree in Europe. In September 1865, a desperate Dostoevsky turned to Mikhail Katkov, the editor of the journal *Russian Herald* and his former ideological rival, to pitch his idea for *Crime and Punishment*.

The idea of the story … is the psychological account of a certain crime.

The action is contemporary, set in the present year. A young man, expelled from the university … living in extreme poverty … having succumbed to certain strange "unfinished" ideas floating in the air, has resolved to get out of his nasty situation all at once … to kill a certain old woman … who lends money at interest. The old woman is stupid, deaf, ill, greedy, charges yidlike interest, is evil and eats up others' lives, torturing her young sister who works as her maid. "She is good for nothing," "why is she alive?" … These questions confuse the young man. He resolves to kill and rob her; to bring happiness to his mother living in the provinces; to save his sister, living as a companion in the home of some landowners, from the lascivious advances of the head of this landowning family—advances that threaten her with ruin; to finish his studies, go abroad, and then all his life to be honest, firm, steadfast in performing "his humane duty to humankind," by which he will certainly "expiate his crime" …

Although such crimes are terribly difficult to carry out … completely by chance he succeeds in accomplishing his undertaking quickly and successfully.

He spends almost a month after this until the final catastrophe. There is no suspicion of him, and there cannot be. Here's where the whole psychological process of the crime unfolds. Unresolved questions confront the murderer, unforeseen and unexpected feelings torment his heart. God's truth and earthly law take their toll, and he ends up *forced* by himself to turn himself in. Forced, even if he perishes in prison, at least to be reunited with people. The feeling of disconnection and dissociation from humankind, which he feels immediately upon committing the crime, have tormented him. The law of truth and human nature have taken their toll [text unclear]. The criminal himself decides to accept suffering in order to expiate his deed. (28/2:136)

Although Dostoevsky was anxious about approaching him, Katkov was a practical editor and his journal needed good writers. He sent Dostoevsky an advance. When *Crime and Punishment* began serialization in 1866, it was an instant success. Dostoevsky subsequently published *The Idiot* (1868), *Demons* (1871–72), and *The Brothers Karamazov* (1879–80) in the *Russian Herald*.

In October 1866, while serializing *Crime and Punishment*, Dostoevsky had to take a month's break to meet a strict deadline required to retain the rights to his published work, including *Crime and Punishment*. To write *The Gambler*, an extraordinary novella about gambling addiction written while Dostoevsky was still a gambling addict,[3] Dostoevsky took a different gamble and hired a young stenographer, Anna Grigorievna Snitkina. Shortly after meeting his deadline, Dostoevsky proposed to Anna, after which they married and moved to Europe to escape his creditors.

During the next four years (1867–71), the Dostoevskys moved often. In 1867, they spent several months in Baden-Baden, the gambling resort where Dostoevsky famously quarrelled with Ivan Turgenev (1818–83), before moving to Geneva, where their first daughter Sophia was born and, after three short months, died (1868). The heartbroken pair moved to Vevey and then to Florence, where Dostoevsky finished *The Idiot*. They next moved to Dresden, where their daughter Lyubov was born in 1869. That year, after reading about a student murdered by the revolutionary Sergei Nechaev and his co-conspirators, Dostoevsky began work on *Demons*, which began serialization in 1871, the year the Dostoevskys returned to Petersburg and their son Fyodor was born.

In 1873, Dostoevsky plunged back into the journalistic world as editor of *The Citizen*, a weekly periodical published by the conservative Prince Vladimir Meshchersky. There Dostoevsky began his "Diary of a Writer" as a column. In 1874, he quit the paper to write *The Adolescent*, which began serialization in

---

3   Richard J. Rosenthal, "Gambling," in *Dostoevsky in Context*, ed. Deborah A. Martinsen and Olga Maiorova (Cambridge: Cambridge University Press, 2015), 148–56.

the liberal journal *Fatherland Notes* in 1875, the year their son Alexei was born. Dostoevsky then returned to journalism as sole writer, editor, and publisher of the monthly *Diary of a Writer* (1876–77, 1880, 1881), which enjoyed wide popularity with readers across the political spectrum. In May 1878, Alexei (age three) died suddenly of epilepsy, and Dostoevsky, grief-stricken, visited the Optina Pustyn monastery, along with the philosopher Vladimir Solovyov, where he met twice with the Elder Amvrosy, who became a prototype for the Elder Zosima in *The Brothers Karamazov* (1879–81). Dostoevsky's final novel cemented his national reputation and later secured his international fame. From the depths of prison under Nicholas I, Dostoevsky thus rose to the heights of fame under Alexander II. His funeral in February 1881 was a major public event, with thousands attending.

CRIME AND PUNISHMENT AS A PRODUCT OF ITS TIME

Like most major nineteenth-century Russian novels, *Crime and Punishment* was first printed serially in a "thick" journal, that is, a compendium of literary, philosophical, economic, political, scientific, and journalistic content published monthly. Since Russia's government provided few outlets for public engagement, and since Russia's bureaucratic censorship drove much political thinking into literature and criticism, journals became sites of education and cultural formation as well as ideological partisanship and contention.

In the 1840s–50s, the major journalistic battles were fought between Slavophiles and Westernizers. Slavophiles pursued national renewal in Russian institutions (especially the peasant commune) and held that Russia's cultural uniqueness derived from the Christian faith preserved by the Russian people. Westernizers criticized Russia's backwardness and urged Russia to emulate Western Europe's civic institutions and rule of law. Despite ideological differences, the two groups supported freedom of speech and abolition of serfdom.

After Nicholas I's death in 1855, censorship loosened, a new era of *glasnost'* (openness) emerged, and "thick" journals proliferated. Before ideological battle lines were drawn, some journals, including the Dostoevsky brothers' *Time* and *Epoch*, offered synthetic, intermediary positions. The Dostoevskys' journals articulated and promoted *pochvennichestvo*, an ideology of Russianness rooted in the soil that advocated closing the gap between the largely Western-educated classes, most of whom had become alienated from the Russian soil, and the uneducated but Christ-bearing Russian people. Such a union occurs in *Crime and Punishment*, when Raskolnikov, who suffers from Western ideas, returns to Christian values through his love for Sonya.

By the mid-1860s, the issues had changed, positions had polarized, all middle ground had disappeared, and censorship regulations changed regularly. The journals on the far left, the *Contemporary* (1812–62) and the *Russian Word* (1859–66), became the organs of radical critics, who articulated an ideology of positivism, scientism, socialism, and feminism, combined with the rejection of autocracy, religion, and tradition—an ideology then called "nihilism."[4] The term "nihilism" was first used by Ivan Turgenev in his 1862 novel *Fathers and Sons*, whose protagonist Bazarov declares that his generation would demolish the present in order to build the future on more solid foundations. Thereafter the term "nihilism" designated both rebellious behavior and ideologies that ran counter to prevailing social norms, institutions, and beliefs. As the historian Derek Offord points out, the designation "nihilism" was a misnomer, as radical youth were far from believing in nothing: they placed great hope in the power of natural science to improve human life and were driven by a concern for those less privileged.[5] Although critical of nihilist ideology, Dostoevsky believed that most young radicals had altruistic motives.

Crime and Punishment was conceived and written in the mid-1860s, a period when journals not only proliferated, but also vied for the same readers and authors as their competitors, the daily newspapers, which printed more copies and addressed a broader spectrum of readers.[6] Both Dostoevsky's novel and Raskolnikov's article are products of this thriving print culture. Dostoevsky's novel was published in the successful, somewhat conservative "thick" journal *Russian Herald*; Raskolnikov's article, which draws much of its language from nihilist journals, appeared in the fictional *Periodical Discourse*, probably a minor newspaper, as they tended "to publish especially daring articles by novice authors like Raskolnikov."[7]

Throughout the 1860s and 1870s, print media thrived and avidly reported on the judicial reforms. Dostoevsky had been tried and sentenced under the

---

4   Robert L. Belknap, "Survey of Russian Journals, 1840–1880," in *Literary Journals in Imperial Russia*, ed. Deborah A. Martinsen (Cambridge: Cambridge University Press, 1997), 106.

5   Derek Offord, "Nihilism and Terrorism," in Martinsen and Maiorova, *Dostoevsky in Context*, 49.

6   Konstantine Klioutchkine, "Modern Print Culture," in Martinsen and Maiorova, *Dostoevsky in Context*, 221–28.

7   Konstantine Klioutchkine, "The Rise of *Crime and Punishment* from the Air of the Media," *Slavic Review* 61, no. 1 (Spring 2002): 107.

pre-reform judicial system, which was largely inquisitorial, based on statutes dictated from above and implemented behind closed doors. The court reform (1864) introduced a more European system with an independent judiciary and adversarial procedures that allowed a plaintiff and defendant (for civil suits) or a prosecutor and defense lawyer (for criminal suits) to present their cases before a judge and jury. Trials were open to the public, proceedings were published in the press, and a professional legal class came into being.[8] In 1860, the new position of judicial investigator, held by Porfiry Petrovich in *Crime and Punishment*, was introduced. Judicial investigators enjoyed considerable independence and authority: they could interrogate victims, suspects, and witnesses; collect material evidence; search premises; and arrest suspects. Dostoevsky's Porfiry Petrovich, like many other fictional judicial investigators of this time, is portrayed as a figure of authority, intelligence, professionalism, and humanity.[9] In Dostoevsky's novel, Porfiry works for the salvation of Raskolnikov's soul as well as for the reduction of his sentence.

CRIME AND PUNISHMENT AS A PETERSBURG TEXT

Dostoevsky sets his novel in St. Petersburg, Peter the Great's "window on the West." With autocratic power and iron will, Peter constructed his planned city on inhospitable marshland at great human cost. Peter's defenders praised him as a world builder; his opponents called him the Antichrist. Thus was born a myth of duality that encompassed both city and tsar. By the time Dostoevsky began his writing career, Alexander Pushkin and Nikolai Gogol had already immortalized St. Petersburg's duality in verse and prose. Pushkin's narrative poem, "The Bronze Horseman" (1833), transformed the original myth of the city's founding as a cosmic battle between order and chaos into a historic flood, which pitted nature (the elements) against culture (the granite city). The poem dramatizes the revolt of a humble clerk against the imperial, impersonal state, symbolized by Falconet's statue of Peter the Great. Pushkin portrays Peter not as creator or destroyer, but as both, thereby establishing the tradition of the Petersburg text, which holds antithetic elements in tension. Gogol's

---

8   Richard Wortman, "The Great Reforms and the New Courts," in Martinsen and Maiorova, *Dostoevsky in Context*, 13–21.

9   Claire Whitehead, *The Poetics of Early Russian Crime Fiction, 1860–1917: Deciphering Stories of Detection* (Cambridge: Modern Humanities Research Association, 2018), 5, 55.

Petersburg stories focus more on the city as Russia's administrative and social capital, highlighting the division between punctilious officialdom and the uncanny. Dostoevsky evokes his predecessors' contributions, adding psychological and philosophical depth, first with his novella *The Double* (1846), then with *Crime and Punishment*. Like Dickens and Balzac before him, Dostoevsky makes his city emblematic of Western urban civilization. As the site of Russia's self-consciousness vis-à-vis the West, Petersburg is also an apt setting for Raskolnikov's divided self.

SOME NOTES ON NAMES

Rodion Romanovich Raskolnikov. The root "**rod**," which denotes family and kinship, embeds the idea of relatedness into his first name. His patronymic **Romanovich** (son of Roman) evokes both the Romanov dynasty (1613–1917) and the novel/**roman** (making him son of the novel). **Raskolnikov** derives from the verb *raskolot'* (to cleave, split) and evokes the *raskolniki* (schismatics), a group of religious dissenters who left the Russian Orthodox Church in 1666, an event known as the Schism (*Raskol*). In his journalism, Dostoevsky characterized ideological divisions among young 1860s radicals as a *raskol* (schism). The name marks Dostoevsky's protagonist as a modern, divided self.

The Raskolnikovs are all remarkably good-looking; Raskolnikov's mother is **Pulcheria**, from the Latin word *pulcher* (beautiful, morally excellent). His sister is **Avdotya**, known by the diminutive form of her name, Dunya, from the Greek *eudokia* (well-seeming, good opinion).

Semyon Zakharovich Marmeladov. Marmelad, a flat, sugar-coated jelly candy, suggests saccharine spinelessness.

Sonya, Marmeladov's daughter from his first marriage, is the diminutive for Sophia, from the Greek word meaning "holy wisdom," revered in Eastern Orthodoxy as an intermediary between the divine and humankind.

Svidrigailov, not a Russian name, was based on a historical figure called Svidrigailo, whose character and deeds were similarly debauched.

Porfiry Petrovich. *Porfira* (purple) is the color both of royal garments and of Sunday or Easter vestments, perhaps suggesting Porfiry's dual roles as civil servant and secular priest. References to **Peter**, including the patronymics **Petrovich** and **Petrovna**, evoke not only Peter the Great, who set Russia on a westernizing, modernizing path that divided the educated classes from the Russian people, but also Peter the apostle.

Luzhin's name derives from *luzha* or "puddle." It is also suggestive of the German verb *lügen* (to lie) and the Russian equivalent *lgat'* (*lgu, lzhesh'*).[10] His name and patronymic, **Petr Petrovich**, imply a double dose of unhealthy Western influences.

Razumikhin's last name derives from the noun ***razum*** or "reason" (similar to German *Vernunft*), often connoting common sense, and the verb *vrazumit'*, "to bring someone to his senses." The noun *rassudok* (similar to German *Verstand*) is also translated "reason," but *rassudok* signifies a more limited, calculating kind of thinking. In Dostoevsky's work, *razum* has positive connotations, and *rassudok*, negative ones. Razumikhin's first name, **Dmitry** (from Demeter, "earth"), hints at his healthy connection with earthly life.

---

10 Carol Apollonio, *Dostoevsky's Secrets: Reading Against the Grain* (Evanston, IL: Northwestern University Press, 2009), 87.

CHAPTER 2

Overview

*C*rime and Punishment gains much of its power by dramatizing Raskolnikov's alienation and search for identity. On leave from university, Raskolnikov commits a murder that nearly defies explanation, but, ultimately, is motivated by ideas prevailing in the intellectual climate. These ideas inexorably clash with Raskolnikov's inmost heart, his conscience. To engage readers both cognitively and emotionally, Dostoevsky devises an innovative narrative strategy that stages the collision between Raskolnikov's reason and feeling, his rationality and moral emotion. We know Raskolnikov is a murderer, but we still want him to get away—at least initially.

NARRATIVE STRATEGY

Dostoevsky implicates readers in his novel's ethical action by employing a narrative strategy that manipulates our perspective and exploits our emotions. Dostoevsky began *Crime and Punishment* as a first-person narrative but changed it to third-person, retaining the advantages of each. Dostoevsky's narrator both creates sympathy for his murderer-protagonist by revealing his thoughts and feelings from the inside (first-person advantage) and distances readers from him by offering outsider commentary and perspective (third-person advantage).

Dostoevsky exploits readers' emotions by creating the expectation of a guilt script—crime, repentance, punishment, expiation—yet offering us a shame scenario, which has no fixed script. Shame relates broadly to human identity and entails negative evaluation of a person's whole self, arising from feelings of inferiority, inadequacy, or exclusion. Guilt pertains more narrowly to human action and entails transgression against personal, moral, social, or legal norms. While guilt involves temporary, voluntary actions that one can expiate, shame is a more permanent state connected to one's being in the world. We may feel guilty for harming another, but we feel shame that we are the kind of person who would do so.[1] Moreover, in guilt one is the agent of an action, whereas in shame one is the object.[2] Shame is thus experienced passively, which accounts for much of the pain it evokes.

In *Crime and Punishment*, Dostoevsky activates readers' emotions by revealing characters' emotions. Contemporary research has shown that emotion works as a process: it starts with an automatic, non-cognitive evaluation that triggers a physiological response followed by a cognitive evaluation of that response.[3] The three key components are instant judgment, physical response, and mental evaluation. Long before this research, Dostoevsky exploited this process, using the dual action of emotion and evaluation to involve readers in the action of his texts. Since moral emotions entail judgments that identify what we care about and thus value, they awaken our cognitive as well as affective capacities. By portraying characters experiencing emotions, Dostoevsky not only allows readers to understand who the characters are and what they care about, he also makes us experience and reflect on their emotions. In short, Dostoevsky engages readers' emotions, then pushes us into cognitive overdrive. In an unexpected yet powerful way, Dostoevsky's texts mimic the process of emotion itself.

By immersing us in Raskolnikov's experiences in *Crime and Punishment*, Dostoevsky engages readers viscerally. By identifying Raskolnikov with nihilist ideology and language, Dostoevsky engages us ideologically. By posing eternal questions of good and evil, justice and inequality, freedom and moral responsibility, Dostoevsky engages us in the struggle for Raskolnikov's soul. Dostoevsky's novel thus touches on all the burning social, political, and metaphysical issues of his day—and our own.

By the end of part 1, Raskolnikov has committed two heinous murders— leaving readers, and even Raskolnikov himself, asking why. The novel suggests many possible motives, including his theory of the extraordinary man (a staple of journalistic discourse in the 1860s). This book argues that Raskolnikov uses the extraordinary man theory to hide his shame at being dependent on the women in his life and then develops an emotion-based litmus test for himself:

---

1   Deborah A. Martinsen, *Surprised by Shame: Dostoevsky's Liars and Narrative Exposure* (Columbus, OH: Ohio State University Press, 2003), 1–17.

2   Gunnar Karlsson and Lennart Sjobert, "The Experience of Guilt and Shame: A Phenomenological-Psychological Study," *Human Studies* 32, no. 3 (September 2009): 352.

3   Jenefer Robinson, *Deeper Than Reason: Emotion and Its Role in Literature, Music, and Art* (Oxford: Clarendon Press, 2005), 59.

no guilt signifies strength; guilt signifies weakness, which is shameful. For Raskolnikov to admit guilt would thus expose his shame. Although Raskolnikov finally confesses to his crime, he evinces no signs of the repentance necessary for a guilt script until the Epilogue's last pages. Dostoevsky thus keeps readers off-balance for the novel's duration—we continually expect, but do not get, a guilt script. Dostoevsky effects this strategy by keeping the guilt script alive among the novel's characters. Because most characters view Raskolnikov as a moral agent, they expect him to feel concern for others and to act accordingly. Since readers share characters' expectations, when Raskolnikov does not comply, their puzzlement becomes ours. As characters "read" Raskolnikov— his face, his words, his actions—trying to understand what motivates him, readers follow suit. The discrepancy between what we expect and what we witness keeps us both involved and uncertain. Dostoevsky thus makes us interpret, evaluate, and decide for ourselves—the goal of a liberal arts education.

CLOSE READING: LESSONS IN NARRATIVE

A close reading of the novel's first six paragraphs provides a good sense of how Dostoevsky uses point of view, direct and indirect discourse, and the roles of author and narrator. It also offers readers first glimpses of Raskolnikov's shame.

The first paragraph, a single sentence, supplies time, protagonist, place: "In the beginning of July, during an extreme heat wave, toward evening, a young man exited the closet he rented from tenants in S— Lane, stepped out to the street and slowly, as though undecided, headed toward the K— Bridge." As Margo Shohl notes, local time is also biblical time: the novel's first two words—*V nachale* (In the beginning)—cite the first words of the Gospel of John, which cites the first words of Genesis.[4] Likewise, the novel's time evokes Aristotle's unity of time: the **beginning** of a **middle** month (July) toward the **end** of day. By combining literary, biblical, and local time, Dostoevsky cannily inscribes arcs of tragedy and salvation into his realistic novel.

By calling the protagonist's rented lodging a "closet," the narrator signals his protagonist's poverty and hints that he lives in Petersburg, where rental buildings were common. By using abbreviations (S— Lane and K— Bridge) to designate locations, he employs a standard Russian literary practice that signifies typicality. Since Moscow and provincial towns were organized differently,

---

4   Margo Shohl, "Teaching *Crime and Punishment*, Step by Step" (lecture presented to the Literature Humanities faculty, Columbia University, New York, April 2013).

these designations allowed Dostoevsky's contemporaries to locate the young man in Petersburg, information the narrator withholds until paragraph six. This opening paragraph raises more questions than it answers: why is the young man walking slowly, why is he undecided, where is he going?

In the second paragraph, the narrator shifts from description to explanation. He first provides external facts that reinforce the novel's realism—the young man's "closet" is more like an "armoire" than an "apartment"; it is under the roof of a five-story (thus rental) building; his landlady lives one floor down; her door is almost always open. While noting that the young man "had successfully evaded a meeting with his landlady on the stairs" in the first sentence, the narrator only reports his emotions at paragraph's end: "And each time the young man passed by, he felt some kind of fevered and cowardly sensation, which made him wince with shame. He was indebted to his landlady, and he was afraid to meet her." This explanation both introduces the young man's shame and anticipates the information about his debts to other women: the old pawnbroker, his mother, and his sister.

In paragraph three, the narrator moves further into his protagonist's head, first reporting omnisciently, then allowing readers access to his thoughts using free indirect discourse, that is, by citing his thoughts without quotation marks. The first four sentences report and analyze his protagonist's isolation and indifference. The last clause, "and he didn't want to deal with" (his daily affairs), however, uses indirect discourse to shift perspective from narrator to character. Dostoevsky's narrator then allows readers to overhear the young man talking to himself: "Basically, he was not afraid of any landlady, whatever she might be, plotting against him."

After briefly resuming omniscience in paragraph four, the narrator plunges us back into the young man's head in paragraph five by reporting his thoughts directly: "'I want to attempt such a thing and at the same time I fear such trifles'—he thought with a strange smile." The ensuing inner monologue (signaled by quotation marks) reveals that the young man senses incongruities between his plan and his fears. Readers also see his preoccupation with the thought of originality, a concern that would have marked him as a cliché, one of many 1860s university students-turned-journalists fixated on the questions "'who am I?' and 'what is my new word?'"[5] Early in the novel, Dostoevsky thus debunks Raskolnikov's supposed originality for contemporary readers.

---

5   Konstantine Klioutchkine, "Modern Print Culture," in Martinsen and Maiorova, *Dostoevsky in Context* (Cambridge: Cambridge University Press, 2015), 224.

In paragraph six, the narrator reveals that we are in Dostoevsky's Petersburg. The young man does not live amidst the city's grand boulevards with their classical architecture, but in a crowded, stifling, dusty, smelly street full of taverns. We learn that he is "remarkably good looking," grimaces disgust at his surroundings, and then forgets about them—"not noticing his surroundings, and even not wanting to notice them." This last phrase echoes the earlier statement "he didn't want to deal with them," signaling the narrator's re-entry into his protagonist's head, an oscillation between outside and inside that persists for the rest of the paragraph, indeed, for the rest of the novel.

Close reading of these opening paragraphs reveals how Dostoevsky's narrator skillfully weaves in and out of his protagonist's head, blurring the boundary between narrative and character perspective. But we must also consider the difference between narrator and author. The author creates the novel's fictional world: he invents Raskolnikov (whose name we learn in paragraph 11) and the other characters, sets the novel in Petersburg, determines the plot, sets the themes, chooses its polemics, and structures the text. When I refer to "Dostoevsky," I mean Dostoevsky the author. Dostoevsky also creates a selectively omniscient narrator who describes the characters, reports their thoughts, speeches, and interactions, and offers occasional observations.[6] As readers, we are members of both the author's and the narrator's audiences. As members of the narrative audience, we experience the text's action along with the characters. As members of the authorial audience, we experience the text's action while remaining aware that the novel is a fictional construct.[7] In the authorial audience, we thus enjoy the intellectual engagement and double consciousness that provide the text's aesthetic pleasure.

In *Crime and Punishment*, Dostoevsky maximizes our immersion as narrative audience in parts 1 and 2, after which he presses hard on our role as authorial audience, providing the distance we need to engage in the text's ethical action. In short, Dostoevsky deploys a both/and narrative strategy: he uses his narrator's proximity to Raskolnikov's point of view to create sympathy for him (our position in the narrative audience), and he offers us the perspective necessary to separate the act of murder from the heart of the murderer (our position in the authorial audience). We experience horror at the crime yet root for the murderer to escape. We know it's a fiction, but it feels real.

---

6   Gary Rosenshield, *"Crime and Punishment": The Techniques of the Omniscient Author* (Lisse, Netherlands: Peter de Ridder Press, 1978), 26–37.

7   Peter Rabinowitz, *Before Reading: Narrative Conventions and the Politics of Interpretation* (Ithaca, NY: Cornell University Press, 1987), 93–104.

PLOT

In part 1, Raskolnikov visits the pawnbroker for a trial run (chapter 1); he then stops at a tavern and hears Marmeladov's drunken speech, which introduces most of the novel's major social justice and metaphysical themes, offers the novel's first confession, and directs attention to the moral emotions and virtues that accompany the human condition (chapter 2). Raskolnikov's mother's letter (chapter 3) outlines his family's economic circumstances, underscoring social justice and women's issues. Raskolnikov responds to the letter with both an inner monologue and an external attempt to rescue a young girl on the street (chapter 4). Raskolnikov's dream of the mare introduces his moral conscience (chapter 5). In addition to dramatizing Raskolnikov's horror and guilt at the thought of murder, the dream of the mare highlights the difference between two kinds of dream—the unconscious dream (*son*) of the mare and the conscious daydream (*mechta*) of murder. These opening chapters create sympathy for Raskolnikov by highlighting his generosity, love of family, sensitivity to power relations and social injustice, and horror at the idea of murder; they also reveal glimpses of his alienation, egoism, and rational calculating. By devoting so many pages to the planned murder of the pawnbroker and so few paragraphs to the unplanned murder of her half-sister Lizaveta (chapter 7), the narrator anticipates the divide in characters' thinking about the crime: Raskolnikov and most of the novel's male characters focus on the pawnbroker's murder, whereas Nastasya, Sonya, and Dunya all remind us of Lizaveta's. This divide, in turn, reveals one of Dostoevsky's narrative strategies—he links the pawnbroker's murder to Raskolnikov's theory (focus on shame) and portrays Lizaveta's murder as its unintended consequence (focus on guilt). Finally, by ending part 1 with the murders and Raskolnikov's fortuitous escape, Dostoevsky establishes the novel's focus on the crime's *whydunit*.

Part 2 creates and thwarts readers' expectation of a guilt script, revealing how Raskolnikov's moral and physical punishment begins, how the cast of characters expands, and how close the narrator remains to Raskolnikov. It includes Raskolnikov's visit to the police station (chapter 1), his experiences of receiving alms on the Nikolaevsky bridge, Nastasya's diagnosis, "It's the blood" (chapter 2), Razumikhin's role in his recovery (chapters 3 and 4), Luzhin's first visit (chapter 5), Raskolnikov's near confession to Zamyotov in the tavern, Marmeladov's death (chapter 6), and the arrival of Raskolnikov's family (chapter 7).

In part 3 the narrator's focus widens to include other characters' perceptions of Raskolnikov—Razumikhin describes him as a divided self (chapter 2), the young medical student Zosimov notes Raskolnikov's self-knowledge and prescribes a return to the university (chapter 3), and Raskolnikov's sister Dunya observes that her brother is playacting (chapter 3). Part 3 also features Raskolnikov's first visit to Porfiry Petrovich, the judicial investigator, and the discussion of Raskolnikov's article on crime (chapter 5). Part 3 ends with Raskolnikov's puzzling unconscious dream of a failed murder (chapter 6).

Part 4, the novel's literal and figurative center, contains many highly charged scenes—Raskolnikov's first meeting with Svidrigailov (chapter 1), Dunya's expulsion of Luzhin (chapter 2), Raskolnikov's first visit to Sonya and its dramatic gospel reading (chapter 4), Raskolnikov's second visit to Porfiry (chapter 5), Mikolka's unexpected confession (chapter 6), and the visit from the man "from under the earth" (chapter 6). Here Dostoevsky knits his themes together more tightly—Raskolnikov worries that Svidrigailov may be part of his dream, introducing the theme of epistemic uncertainty. Luzhin reveals his egoism and drive for power, vindicating Raskolnikov's moral intuition that he is a predatory male. Sonya's recitation of Lazarus's story from the Gospel of John hints at the possibility of Raskolnikov's resurrection. Raskolnikov's second visit to Porfiry highlights the novel's detective story component. Mikolka's unexpected confession reinforces the theme of confession and reminds us that Raskolnikov promised to tell Sonya who killed Lizaveta (another confession). Part 4 closes with the man "from under the earth" (chapter 7), whose visit not only evokes the theme of earthly and divine forgiveness raised by Marmeladov (part 1, chapter 2) but reminds Raskolnikov both of his crime (guilt) and his fear of being exposed (shame).

Part 5 continues Dostoevsky's project of moving readers out of Raskolnikov's head by focusing on others (Luzhin, chapter 1; Katerina Ivanovna, chapter 2) and by crafting two Marmeladov family scandals: one inside the Marmeladov living space (chapter 3), one on the streets of St. Petersburg (chapter 5). These scandals frame Raskolnikov's wordless confession to Sonya and his wordy attempts to explain his motives to her (chapter 4). As Sonya repeatedly rejects his explanations on moral grounds, Dostoevsky offers readers further distance from Raskolnikov's perspective.

In part 6, Dostoevsky stages a series of farewell meetings that reveal multiple connections among characters. Raskolnikov must choose between confession (Sonya and Porfiry) and escape (Svidrigailov). This part stages Svidrigailov's dark night of the soul as a prelude to his suicide. It also dramatizes the breakdown of Raskolnikov's theory-encrusted shell, his emotional reconnection to others, and his verbal confession to the police.

The novel's Epilogue, with its change of narration and happy ending, continues to provoke controversy. Critics complain of its artificiality; defenders argue for its organic connection to the novel. In part 1 of the Epilogue, the narrator adopts an impersonal, omniscient style, summarizing the events of the eighteen months following Raskolnikov's confession. In part 2 the narrator returns his focus to Raskolnikov and recapitulates the novel's events in condensed yet modified form: instead of stepping over a moral law and committing a crime, Raskolnikov steps into a new life and experiences a rebirth in love. Because Dostoevsky has identified Sonya so closely with Lizaveta, who is associated with the guilt script, Raskolnikov's acknowledgment of the suffering he has caused Sonya and his intention to redeem it demonstrate, on the novel's very last page, that he is ready to accept responsibility for his crimes. On this reading, Dostoevsky waits until the very last page of *Crime and Punishment* to give readers the guilt script we have been expecting all along.

TEACHING TIPS

To understand how Dostoevsky fuses psychology and ideology, I use four big questions to structure class discussions:

- How does Dostoevsky's narration work?
- Why do most readers root for the murderer-protagonist to escape the scene of the crime?
- Why do most characters (and thus most readers) forget Lizaveta, the second murder victim?
- Is the Epilogue organic or artificial?

I also recommend an in-class focus on Raskolnikov's dreams:

- part 1, chapter 5—dream of the mare;
- part 3, chapter 6—dream of killing the pawnbroker again;
- Epilogue—trichinae dreams;

and confessions or near confessions:

- part 1, chapter 6—taunting Zamyotov;
- part 4, chapter 3—nonverbal communication to Razumikhin with his eyes;

- part 4, chapter 4—promising to tell Sonya;
- part 4, chapter 5—almost telling Porfiry;
- part 5, chapter 4—conveying guilt to Sonya;
- part 6, chapter 7—acknowledging crime to Dunya;
- part 6, chapter 8—fully confessing at police station.

TEACHING PART 1

There are two basic strategies for teaching part 1 of *Crime and Punishment* that depend on the syllabus time allotted. If students have not read all of part 1 for the first class, go sequentially and thematically. If they have, close read the novel's first six paragraphs (see above) and then jump directly to the murder scene (chapter 7) and discuss why most readers root for Raskolnikov to get away.

While some students feel nothing but revulsion for our young axe-murderer, most feel sympathy for him which they justify by arguing that Raskolnikov is a divided self, whose rational thinking conflicts with his moral emotions. They claim that he is a good guy at heart. Most importantly, they cite textual evidence to support this view: Raskolnikov's charity to the Marmeladovs (chapter 2), his love for his family (chapter 4), his attempt to rescue the young girl from a predatory older man (chapter 4), and his dream of the mare (chapter 5). In short, Raskolnikov's spontaneous actions and thoughts establish his moral core.

Next, discuss the evidence against Raskolnikov—the selfish rationalizations that negate his spontaneous impulses to help the Marmeladovs (they have Sonya, chapter 2) and the young girl (she's just a statistic, chapter 4), his superstitions (chapters 5 and 6), and the murders—one calculated, one unplanned (chapter 7). Finally, discuss Dostoevsky's narrative ace-in-the-hole—how his narrator uses the same language and imagery to describe both Lizaveta's fear of being killed and Raskolnikov's fear of being caught, transforming the escaping murderer into a trapped quarry (chapter 7). The rapid shift away from Raskolnikov's second act of murder to his fear of being caught leaves readers no time to think. By having us crouch with bated breath behind the door with Raskolnikov, Dostoevsky makes readers complicit in his escape.

This leap from the novel's opening to Raskolnikov's get-away induces students to identify major moments and themes in the intervening chapters, thereby generating their own insights about my first two questions—how the narration works and why we root for Raskolnikov to get away with murder. Thereafter, we move sequentially and thematically—like instructors who teach the novel more slowly.

CHAPTER 3

Parts 1 and 2:
Getting Away with Murder

THE MARMELADOVS:
CONFESSION, SOCIAL JUSTICE, PARALLEL PLOTS

Like Shakespeare, Dostoevsky often places words of great thematic import in the mouths of minor characters, or even fools. In part 1, chapter 2 we meet Semyon Zakharych Marmeladov, who delivers the novel's first confession. Since confession becomes thematic, it is important to understand how it works. In an institutionalized setting, the confessee acknowledges wrongdoing to a confessor, who is an authority figure. In a religious setting, the confessor can offer acceptance and forgiveness, sometimes asking the confessee to perform an act of expiation. In a legal setting, the confessor may instigate judicial proceedings. In this novel, we must ask why Dostoevsky has Marmeladov drunkenly confess to an impoverished student in a seedy tavern with others mocking him. Why is Marmeladov's story important? What makes Raskolnikov a good target audience?

Marmeladov's phrase "nowhere to go" offers an answer. Marmeladov says he married Katerina Ivanovna because "I could not look at such suffering. You may judge thereby what degree her calamities had reached, if she, well-educated, well-bred, from a well-known family, agreed to marry me! But she did! ... For she had nowhere to go. Do you understand, do you understand, my dear sir, what it means when there is indeed nowhere else to go?" Marmeladov's iterated phrase sums up the novel's emerging social justice themes—poverty, inequality, and women's limited economic options—themes that will resonate not only in the Raskolnikov family story (chapter 3), but also in the rest of the novel. Dostoevsky thus uses the Marmeladovs to identify systemic problems: the Russian economy was largely family-based and offered no social safety net for the poor. Marmeladov's repeated phrase "nowhere to go" highlights the desperation caused by poverty and points to the era's gender dynamics: women were almost entirely dependent on their families for support. The market for their labor was exceedingly limited.[1] Consequently, if their family renounced them, or if the male breadwinner lost his job or died, women and their children had nowhere to go—but onto the streets, which is what Katerina Ivanovna asks Sonya, her stepdaughter, to do.

Marmeladov's bathetic confession also touches on the moral emotions and virtues that accompany or alleviate such human dilemmas—pride, shame, guilt, repentance, compassion, generosity, and forgiveness. In highlighting Marmeladov's shame and guilt, Dostoevsky creates plot parallels with Raskolnikov. Both men have not only failed to support their families, but have also taken money from the women in their lives and spent it on themselves. Consequently, both families are suffering. Marmeladov masochistically revels in confession; Raskolnikov vacillates between defiant justifications and confession.

Finally, Marmeladov's speech provides gritty specifics that haunt the text. He lost his job in the provinces due to a "change of staff," which probably means he was replaced by nepotism. He brought his family to Petersburg, where he found and lost another job, this time due to his drinking. The Marmeladovs consequently live in a walk-through room in a rental apartment; the children have no education; and his daughter Sonya is driven into prostitution. Earlier Sonya had attempted to support the family by working as a seamstress, but when a state councilor (a high-ranking, well-paid civil servant) did not pay for the six shirts she made him, it broke the family economy. After three days of near-starvation, Katerina Ivanovna nagged Sonya into prostitution, accepted thirty silver rubles for this betrayal, then wept with her. The story is Marmeladov's; the details are Dostoevsky's. Behind his character-narrator's back, Dostoevsky evokes the thirty pieces of silver Judas receives for betraying Jesus—a Gospel reference that makes Sonya into a Christ-like figure betrayed into the hands of a procuress by someone close to her. Moreover, Sonya's body is figuratively transformed into food for her family.

Marmeladov responded to his daughter's fall by begging for another chance, working for a month, but then stealing the remaining salary for a drinking spree.

---

1   Barbara Engel, "The 'Woman Question,' Women's Work, and Women's Options," in Martinsen and Maiorova, *Dostoevsky in Context*, 58–65.

Sitting opposite Raskolnikov, he confesses that he received the thirty kopecks (note the thirty) for that evening from Sonya, who "didn't say anything, only looked at me silently … That is not done on earth, but up there … where they feel anguish and weep for people, and don't reproach, don't reproach! And it hurts more, it hurts more, sir, when they don't reproach!" While Dostoevsky evokes Christ, Marmeladov identifies Sonya not only with the compassion of angels, but also with the iconography of the saints, where eyes express spirituality and beauty. At the end of part 4, chapter 4, Raskolnikov tells Sonya that her father's story had made him decide to seek her after his crime—was this the deciding moment? Was Raskolnikov already thinking that he would need the compassion of a self-sacrificing angel? The forgiveness of a Christ-like figure?

Whatever sympathy Marmeladov's self-accusing rhetoric may have generated for him may well dissipate when Raskolnikov brings the drunken Marmeladov home, and readers see the extent of the family's destitution. Raskolnikov is so moved by it that he leaves his remaining coins on the windowsill for them—one of those moments of compassion and spontaneous generosity that leads us to believe in Raskolnikov's moral goodness. Yet the narrator reports Raskolnikov's subsequent regret and utilitarian calculus. Spontaneous generosity followed by rational calculation. Raskolnikov's divided self.

PULCHERIA ALEXANDROVNA'S LETTER: READER RESPONSE AND PARALLEL PLOTS

After hearing Sonya's story (part 1, chapter 2), Raskolnikov receives a letter from his mother, Pulcheria Alexandrovna, relating the story of his sister Dunya (chapter 3). The juxtaposition allows readers to compare the Marmeladov and Raskolnikov families: both mothers willingly sacrifice their daughters, and both daughters willingly sacrifice themselves for their families. Nonetheless, Sonya is meek, has very little education, and is forced to sacrifice herself so that her stepfamily will not starve, whereas Dunya is proud, well-educated, and chooses to sacrifice herself for her brother's career.

In part 1, chapter 4, Raskolnikov's perceptive reading of his mother's letter[2] reveals how his encounter with Marmeladov has shaped his internal discourse—"Do you know, Dunechka, that Sonechka's lot is in no way nastier

---

2   Olga Meerson, "Theorizing vs. Teaching Literary Theory: What Is to Be Done with *Crime and Punishment*?" in *Teaching Nineteenth-Century Russian Literature*, eds. Deborah A. Martinsen, Cathy Popkin, and Irina Reyfman (Boston: Academic Studies Press, 2014), 43–52.

than yours with Mr. Luzhin?" His mother's letter raises "old, painful, long-standing" questions in his heart, causing him an anguish that takes "the form of a terrible, wild, and fantastic question that tormented his heart and mind, irresistibly demanding resolution. And now his mother's letter suddenly struck him like a thunderbolt. Clearly, he now had not to be anguished, not to suffer passively, merely reasoning about unresolvable questions, but to do something without fail, at once, quickly." He remembers Marmeladov's question about "nowhere to go" and realizes that while yesterday's thought had been a "daydream," "now it suddenly appeared … in some new, threatening, and completely unfamiliar form." He looks for a bench to sit down, but "a small adventure" befalls him on the way.

Although a seeming digression, this "small adventure" in part 1, chapter 4 represents another response to his mother's letter. Raskolnikov sees a young girl walking strangely on the sidewalk and then flopping onto a bench. Raskolnikov reads her situation as perceptively as he reads his mother's letter: he surmises that she is drunk, guesses that she has been abused and re-dressed, and observes a predatory male targeting her. Raskolnikov calls the predatory man "Svidrigailov," pities the girl and wants "to do something without fail, at once, quickly," has second thoughts, and uses the language of rights—"Who am I to help? Do I have the right to help?" Then he criticizes contemporary discourse on prostitution—"Every year, they say, a certain percentage has to go … Splendid little words they have, really: they are so reassuring, scientific. … Now, if it were some other word … And what if Dunechka somehow falls into the percentage!" By having Raskolnikov link the young girl, utilitarian discourse, and Dunya associatively, Dostoevsky concretizes the larger social issues of poverty, women's choices, and prostitution. By calling attention to the language that turns individuals into statistics, Dostoevsky shows how words shape perception: when a young girl becomes a statistic and an old pawnbroker becomes a parasite, the consequences can be fatal.

RASKOLNIKOV'S DREAM OF THE MARE

Raskolnikov's dream of the mare in part 1, chapter 5 engenders reader sympathy for him.[3] We quickly realize that Raskolnikov identifies with two of the

---

3   See Liza Knapp, "Teaching Raskolnikov's Dream: Regarding the Pain of Others in the Classroom," in Martinsen, Popkin, and Reyfman, *Teaching Nineteenth-Century Russian Literature*, 82–96.

dream's major figures—young Raskolnikov and the peasant Mikolka; more slowly, we note his identification with the mare. Young Raskolnikov is horrified as Mikolka brutally beats then kills the mare, all while encouraging bystanders to join him on the cart, which is already too heavy for her to pull. Full of pity for the suffering horse, young Raskolnikov runs to her and cries as her eyes are beaten. When she succumbs to death, he embraces "her dead, bloody muzzle and kisses it, kisses her eyes, her lips. ... Then he suddenly jumps up and hysterically throws himself at Mikolka with his little fists" (chapter 5). As his father drags him away, young Raskolnikov asks why they killed the poor horse; his chest tightens, he cannot breathe, and then adult Raskolnikov wakes up in a sweat, full of horror: "Thank God, it was only a dream!"

On the psychological level, Raskolnikov recognizes his identification not just with his younger dream self but also with Mikolka: "Lord!—he exclaimed,—can it be, can it be that I will really take an axe, hit her on the head, and shatter her skull ... that I will slip in sticky, warm blood, break the lock, steal, and tremble; hide, all covered in blood ... with an axe. ... Lord, can it be?" Mikolka embodies Raskolnikov's murderous rage, his pride, his sense of entitlement, and his desire for omnipotence. Mikolka seems angry with the mare because she is old and weak. As he punishes her for it, his violence begets more violence: first he whips her, then he batters her with a wooden shaft, and finally he slays her with a crowbar. Once she is dead, he seems disappointed that there is no further outlet for his rage. Here Dostoevsky offers an advance glimpse of Raskolnikov's rage at not being the extraordinary man he wants to be.

On the thematic level, Mikolka represents the materialist, utilitarian ideology that Dostoevsky's novel rails against: Mikolka's claim that the mare is useless prepares for Raskolnikov's memory of a conversation overheard in a tavern when he was contemplating his crime (chapter 6). As an officer and a student discuss the pawnbroker, the student calls her "stupid," "evil," and "not only of no use but actually harmful to all." By proposing that the pawnbroker be killed and her money be used to help others, the student voices the utilitarian calculus that Raskolnikov later uses to justify her murder. This kind of thinking—that individuals acting in their own interests benefit society—proleptically links Raskolnikov to Dunya's predatory fiancé Luzhin, who expounds such views in part 2 (chapter 5).

On the socio-political level, Mikolka's repeated exclamation that the mare is "my goods" (*moe dobro*) not only asserts his rights as possessor but also reminds Dostoevsky's readers that until five years earlier serfs had been the possessions of landowners. Even in the post-emancipation era, the memory of serfdom's cruelties, including the owner's ability to buy and sell their serfs, to use and abuse their bodies, was still alive. Mikolka's exclamation thus touches on the novel's theme of social injustice. Luzhin figures prominently here, as does Svidrigailov: both men use their social status and money to abuse women who have neither.

On the metaphysical level, Mikolka's choice of the word *dobro* reminds readers of our existential choices—to do good (*dobro*) or evil (*zlo*). Mikolka chooses to torture and kill the good, which he identifies as "mine." In light of his brutality, Mikolka's utilitarian justification rings hollow. What good does he do by killing his own "good"? By revealing Raskolnikov's identification with Mikolka, Dostoevsky exposes the metaphysical costs of Raskolnikov's intended crime.

On the moral level, young Raskolnikov's identification with the mare can be seen as adult Raskolnikov's sympathy for victims of social injustice. His dream thus reveals his dual identification with both victimizer and victim. Unconsciously, Raskolnikov not only recognizes that it is wrong to kill the pawnbroker, but also realizes that doing so will kill part of the good within him. In part 2, the narrator makes the identification explicit: "Undressing and all atremble, like an overdriven horse, he lay on the sofa" (part 2, chapter 2). Later in the novel, Raskolnikov will exclaim, "I killed myself, not the old crone!" (part 5, chapter 4).

Finally, Boris Tikhomirov draws the reader's attention to a doubling that reflects Raskolnikov's divided self. Dostoevsky attributes the name Mikolka, an uncommon nickname for Nikolai, to two characters: the peasant who kills his mare in Raskolnikov's dream and the peasant who confesses to the pawnbroker's murder (part 4, chapter 6).[4] Mikolka the mare murderer has lost God. Mikolka the innocent painter has a conscience, the sign of God within. Dostoevsky thus doubles down on Raskolnikov's self-division.

TWO KINDS OF DREAM: CONSCIOUS (*MECHTA*) AND UNCONSCIOUS (*SON*)

Moments after waking up from his unconscious dream (*son*), Raskolnikov renounces his conscious dream (*mechta*): "Lord!—he prayed,—show me my way, for I renounce this cursed ... dream of mine!" (chapter 5). Although

---

4   Boris Tikhomirov, *"Lazar! Griadi von": Roman F. M. Dostoevskogo "Prestuplenie i nakazanie" v sovremennom prochtenii. Kniga-kommentarii* (St. Petersburg: Serebrianyi vek, 2005), 111.

I know of no English-language translation that differentiates between the two Russian words, hereafter I use "dream" to designate an unconscious dream (*son*) and "daydream" to designate a conscious, wishful dream (*mechta*). Dostoevsky's narrator introduces Raskolnikov's "terrifying" dream of the mare with a short discourse on unconscious dreams:

> In morbid states, dreams are often distinguished by their unusual distinctness, vividness, and extraordinary resemblance to reality. Sometimes a monstrous picture coalesces, but the setting and the whole process of representation are so credible, with details that are so subtle, unexpected, yet artistically corresponding to the whole picture, that the same dreamer could not invent them in a waking state, even if he were an artist like Pushkin or Turgenev. Such dreams, morbid dreams, are always long remembered and produce a powerful effect on a person's strained and already distressed organism. (Part 1, chapter 5)

Crime and Punishment features two such powerful unconscious dreams—the dream of the mare in part 1 and the dream of the old crone in part 3. This first dream reveals Raskolnikov's moral sensibility—his horror and guilt at the thought of his crime. The second reveals his sense of failure and shame after the fact.

Unlike the unconscious dream of the mare, the daydream that Raskolnikov renounces is conscious—his plan to murder the pawnbroker, Alyona Ivanovna. Already on the novel's third page, Dostoevsky's narrator identifies it as *bezobraznaia*, literally "without form" or "without image." As Robert Jackson keenly observes, Dostoevsky sees the good (moral) and the beautiful (aesthetic) as profoundly interconnected. Throughout his journalistic and fictional writing, Dostoevsky always uses the Russian word *obraz*, which means "form," "shape," or "image," positively. *Obraz* is also the word for "icon" and structures one end of Dostoevsky's aesthetic-moral spectrum, while *bezobrazie*—literally that which is "without image," or shapeless, disfigured, ugly—structures the other end. Since Dostoevsky believed God formed humans in His own image, "all violence against man is a dehumanization—a deformation, finally, of the divine image."[5] By having his narrator use such a morally freighted adjective, Dostoevsky signals authorial judgment on

---

5   Robert Louis Jackson, *Dostoevsky's Quest for Form: A Study of His Philosophy of Art* (New Haven, CT: Yale University Press, 1966), 40–70, esp. 44–58.

Raskolnikov's conscious daydream to murder and thus dehumanize a human being. By juxtaposing conscious and unconscious dreams in part 1, Dostoevsky powerfully exposes Raskolnikov's divided self: his unconscious dream of the mare leads him to renounce his conscious daydream of murder.[6]

GETTING AWAY WITH MURDER

Raskolnikov has clearly been contemplating the old pawnbroker's murder for a long time, and the narrator spends most of part 1, chapter 6 describing how Raskolnikov's rationally planned crime gets haphazardly executed. Raskolnikov oversleeps; the axe he planned to use is unavailable, yet he finds another axe; a hay wagon conceals him as he enters the interior courtyard of the pawnbroker's building; he meets no one on the stairs; and the apartments across from and below the pawnbroker's sit empty. In part 1, chapter 7, the narrator describes both murders briefly—roughly half a page for each murder, one paragraph as lead-in, one as description. He gives the aftermaths more coverage—more than a page for Raskolnikov's fumbling attempts to collect valuables after he kills Alyona Ivanovna, more than half a chapter to Raskolnikov's get-away after killing her half-sister Lizaveta. As we compare the two murders, we note that the pawnbroker raises both hands to her head before the next blows of the axe's blunt edge. Lizaveta raises one hand halfway up, as though to push her attacker away, before the sharp edge falls, a gesture some have seen as an effort to protect her womb, as she is "almost always pregnant" (part 1, chapter 6). Two murders: planned, unplanned; blunt edge, sharp edge; predatory victim, meek victim.

By apportioning much space to the planning and execution of the first murder and little to the second, Dostoevsky's narrator reflects his protagonist's thinking: Raskolnikov almost always thinks about the pawnbroker and hardly at all about Lizaveta. In part 2 and following, many other characters follow suit. This is part of Dostoevsky's strategy—by keeping readers focused on the pawnbroker's murder, he foregrounds Raskolnikov's conscious daydream (the shame script). This keeps readers speculating about Raskolnikov's motives, the novel's central mystery. By providing occasional reminders of Lizaveta (the guilt script), particularly her association with Sonya, Raskolnikov keeps alive the memory of the daydream's unintended consequences and offers further

---

6   In part 3, chapter 2 we learn that conscious daydreams can be plans for the future: Pulcheria Alexandrovna asks Razumikhin what her son's "daydreams" are, and we learn that Razumikhin harbors the "daydream" of marrying Dunya.

evidence of Raskolnikov's ability to repress unwanted thoughts. He also hints that Raskolnikov can redeem himself by accepting responsibility for Lizaveta's murder.

When examining the second murder, we discover the Dostoevskian strategy that explains our desire for Raskolnikov to escape the crime scene: the narrator quickly shifts focus from Lizaveta's murder to Raskolnikov's get-away. Most significantly, he uses the same words to describe Lizaveta's and Raskolnikov's fear. Readers have no time to think about Lizaveta's brutal murder before we experience Raskolnikov's fear of being discovered at the scene of his crime.

Fear dominates the second murder scene. Shaken by the first murder, Raskolnikov is nervously searching the bedroom for the pawnbroker's money, when he hears Lizaveta arrive. The emphases in the following passage are mine:

> **Suddenly** there was the sound of footsteps in the room where the old woman lay. He stopped, **still as death**. But everything was quiet; he must have imagined it. **Suddenly** there came a slight but distinct cry. ... Again there was **dead silence** for a minute or two. He sat crouched by the trunk and waited, **barely breathing**, but **suddenly** jumped up, **seized the axe**, and ran out of the bedroom.
>
> Lizaveta was standing in the middle of the room ... **frozen**, staring at her murdered sister, white as a sheet, and **as if unable to utter a cry**. Seeing him run in, she **trembled like a leaf** ... raised her hand, opened her mouth, **yet still did not utter a cry**, and **slowly began backing away from him** into the corner, staring at him fixedly, point-blank, **but still did not cry out**, as if she did not have the breath to cry out. **He rushed at her with the axe**; she **twisted her lips pitifully, as very small children do** when they begin to be afraid of something, stare at the thing that frightens them, and are on the point of crying out. And this wretched Lizaveta was so simple, so downtrodden, and so permanently frightened that she did not even raise a hand to protect her face, though it would have been the most necessary and natural gesture at that moment. ... She brought her free left hand up very slightly ... and slowly stretched it out toward him as if to keep him away. The blow landed directly on the skull, with the sharp edge, and immediately split the whole upper part of the forehead, almost to the crown. She collapsed. Raskolnikov, utterly at a loss, ... ran to the entry. **Fear was taking hold of him more and more, especially after this second, quite unexpected murder.** (Part 1, chapter 7)

In this short, emotional drama, both protagonists freeze with fear: fear of being killed causes Lizaveta to retreat; fear of being caught causes Raskolnikov to advance. Dostoevsky's narrator conveys their fear so vividly that we see the scene in our mind's eye, as if through a camera lens. This same camera, operated by Dostoevsky's narrator, has been following Raskolnikov since the novel's first page. It is with him as he hears sounds in the next room. It freezes when he freezes, leaps when he leaps, slows while focusing on Lizaveta for five long, detailed sentences, speeds through the murder, and then leaves Lizaveta behind as it refocuses on Raskolnikov and his escape.

In the six-sentence paragraph that introduces this tense scene, the narrator focuses on Raskolnikov and uses the adverb "suddenly" three times, twice as a first word, to convey the murder's unexpectedness. Readers, who have spent seventy-five pages practically inside Raskolnikov's fevered mind, are as unprepared for this murder as Raskolnikov himself.

When focus shifts to Lizaveta, the narrator slows the camera, as those five tightly packed sentences about Lizaveta describe her involuntary reactions—trembling body, open mouth, partially raised hand, twisted lips. The camera slows further as Dostoevsky's narrator editorializes, comparing Lizaveta to a child and thus rousing our compassion. Yet after impersonally describing the rapid, brutal murder, the narrator refocuses on Raskolnikov, deflecting readers' attention away from Lizaveta. During the pawnbroker's premeditated murder, Raskolnikov seems to act "mechanically." During Lizaveta's murder, he seems to act instinctively: it's almost as though he's not there—"The blow fell." In the space of a few pages, we see Raskolnikov transform from a deliberate, albeit nervous, ideological murderer into an unthinking killer.

Yet during the escape scene, most readers, including me, want Raskolnikov to get away.[7] Why? In earlier scenes, Dostoevsky created reader sympathy for Raskolnikov; here he places him in Lizaveta's position. While stepping out of the apartment, Raskolnikov hears footsteps coming up the stairs: "And **suddenly** it seemed to him as though he **had turned to stone**, as though he were in one of those dreams where the dreamer is being pursued, the pursuers are close, **they are going to kill him**, and he is **as if rooted to the spot, unable even**

---

7   As Richard Peace points out, "In literature such direct empathy with the criminal had not been attempted before Dostoevsky. One may cite Macbeth and perhaps other Shakespearean villain/heroes, but for all their soliloquies, they are still figures out there on the stage; they are not in the reader's own mind and there in the room. The space Raskolnikov inhabits is the reader's own personal one." Richard Peace, introduction to *Fyodor Dostoevsky's "Crime and Punishment": A Casebook*, ed. Richard Peace (Oxford: Oxford University Press, 2006), 15.

to move his arms" (emphasis mine)." Like Lizaveta, Raskolnikov is frozen in place "as if ... unable even to move his arms," in contrast to the pawnbroker, who "still managed to raise both hands to her head" as the axe descended.

Dostoevsky's narrator relies on emotional contagion. Before murdering Lizaveta, Raskolnikov freezes, crouched in the next room, **barely breathing**. Standing on the landing, he freezes but then slips back into the apartment, latches the hook, and "**cowered, without breathing**, just at the door." When the coast is finally clear and he runs down the stairs, he hears steps ascending but manages to slip into an empty apartment and "**cowered behind the wall**." The narrator no longer needs to tell us he's barely breathing, for we are barely breathing ourselves. Dostoevsky has caught us—we want the murderer to escape, at least for now. In this way, Dostoevsky makes us *ex post facto* accomplices.[8]

But weren't we already accomplices? Hadn't Dostoevsky already snared some of us intellectually? Don't we all agree that the old pawnbroker is morally repulsive because she profits from others' misery? Don't most of us consider her murder less awful than Lizaveta's? Doesn't the act of reading itself implicate us intellectually, emotionally, or both?

By the end of part 1, Dostoevsky has us where he wants us: most of us are rooting for his sometimes sympathetic young axe-murderer protagonist to escape. Raskolnikov's self-divisions have become ours. Like Raskolnikov waking from his dream of the mare, we are repulsed by the idea of murder, but like him, we are incensed at the many social and economic injustices and angry at the predators we have encountered. We thus understand Raskolnikov's utilitarian justification for murder.

Moreover, like Raskolnikov in part 1, and like Porfiry and others later in the novel, we frequently forget Lizaveta. Dostoevsky's narrator has kept us so close to Raskolnikov that we practically see the novel's events through his eyes. Since he thinks mostly about the pawnbroker, so do we. In order to effect our moral education, Dostoevsky must get us out of Raskolnikov's head. The narrator's third-person perspective will eventually provide us with the opportunity to contextualize and analyze Raskolnikov's thoughts and actions, but not yet.

By the end of part 1, readers should have a grasp of Dostoevsky's narrative strategy, which, as Robert Belknap astutely observes, makes us live intimately with its protagonist for ninety pages, thereby implicating us "in a crime that is vicious, greedy, cold, and despicable. This is the manipulative novel at its

---

8   Robert L. Belknap, *Plots* (New York: Columbia University Press, 2016), 106.

strongest. It tells us what is happening, shows us what is happening, but more than that, it makes us experience what is happening. From the end of part I, the reader, like Raskolnikov, will alternate between a strong drive toward his escape and a drive toward his confession."[9]

Moreover, as we leave part 1, we have seen how Dostoevsky layers his text by evoking intertexts, depicting the socio-economic realities of poverty in 1860s Petersburg, and raising ethical and metaphysical questions. We have seen how he creates parallels between the Marmeladov and Raskolnikov families, thereby casting light on family dynamics and women's economic issues. We have seen how easily his third-person narrator moves in and out of Raskolnikov's head, revealing his conscious daydreams and unconscious dreams, offering us an intellectual justification for murder, taking us with Raskolnikov as he brutally kills two women, and then getting us to root for his escape. As we move forward, aware of Dostoevsky's ability to manipulate our thoughts and feelings, we must ask ourselves what is his goal? Why does he implicate us in Raskolnikov's crime? What lies ahead?

PART 2—THE PUNISHMENT BEGINS

In part 1, Dostoevsky's narrator makes it clear that Raskolnikov's suffering started before the novel's opening pages; in part 2 we see his suffering intensify. For the next three days and eighty pages, readers live through three major forms of Raskolnikov's punishment: illness, isolation, and increasing indecision.

ILLNESS AND DELIRIUM

Part 2 begins and ends in Raskolnikov's room—as he regains and then loses consciousness again. As in part 1, the narrator trains his camera on Raskolnikov. Albeit readers see Raskolnikov from the outside, we have so much access to Raskolnikov's thoughts and emotions that we feel we are inside his fevered brain, riding the disorienting roller coaster of his delirium. Part 2 even opens with Raskolnikov oscillating between remembering "everything" and falling into states of oblivion.

Dostoevsky makes the causes of Raskolnikov's illness as unclear as his motives. Is Raskolnikov feverish because he hasn't eaten for days (part 1, chapter 1), because he committed murder (part 1, chapter 7), or both? Does

---

9   Belknap, *Plots*, 107.

illness engender his crime or accompany it? According to Raskolnikov's theory (part 1, chapter 6), most criminals get caught because they experience an eclipse of reason and failure of will at the critical moment, as though attacked by illness. Yet Raskolnikov himself doesn't know whether illness causes or accompanies crime (chapter 6). This uncertainty keeps readers guessing.

The narrator intensifies our sense of Raskolnikov's delirium by accompanying him as he wanders. His first trip outside lasts six or seven hours and covers much territory: after ten in the morning, he receives a summons; after eleven, he arrives at the police station (where he meets Ilya Petrovich and the young police informant Zamyotov); then he returns to his room, grabs the stolen items, buries them, visits Razumikhin, and receives and rejects alms on the Nikolaevsky Bridge (part 1, chapters 1 and 2).

Arriving unexpectedly at Razumikhin's, Raskolnikov realizes that "I said ... two days ago ... that I'd go see him the day after *that*"—our first clue to Razumikhin's significance. After Razumikhin confirms that his friend is "seriously ill" (chapter 2) and offers him translation work, Raskolnikov accepts it and leaves, only to return and refuse it. This change of mind recalls Raskolnikov's earlier about-face with the young girl on the boulevard, when Raskolnikov first offers the police officer money to help her, then throws up his hands and declares himself unqualified to help. In the case of accepting then rejecting Razumikhin's charity, some readers may speculate that Raskolnikov's ability to give and receive is part of his illness. Or, like Corrigan, some may suspect Razumikhin of trying to control his friend Raskolnikov.[10]

At the end of part 2, chapter 2, Raskolnikov hears Ilya Petrovich beating his landlady. Readers, who experience the beating along with him, only learn that it is an auditory hallucination after he asks Nastasya about it. She stares at him and declares, "It's the blood. ... No one came. It's the blood in you crying out. It's when it has no outlet and the kidneys begin to heat it, and then one imagines things." Nastasya's non-medical diagnosis heightens our awareness of the guilt haunting Raskolnikov's conscience, a further symptom suggesting that the punishment has begun.

Dostoevsky intensifies the readers' sense of Raskolnikov's illness as punishment by expanding the novel's cast of characters. In chapters 1 and 2, many characters confirm that Raskolnikov is ill. As Raskolnikov cycles in and out of consciousness for the next few days, he receives multiple visits—from his

---

10 Yuri Corrigan, *Dostoevsky and the Riddle of the Self* (Evanston, IL: Northwestern University Press, 2017), 25–28.

friend Razumikhin (chapters 3 to 5), the medical student Zosimov (chapter 4), and Raskolnikov's prospective brother-in-law Luzhin (chapter 5). During this period, Raskolnikov awakens as Zosimov and Razumikhin discuss the pawn-broker's murder (chapter 4). Like Raskolnikov, the male characters who discuss the crime focus on the murder of Alyona Ivanovna, the pawnbroker. When Nastasya blurts out that "Lizaveta was killed too!" (chapter 3), she is the novel's first rare reminder of Raskolnikov's unintended murder victim.

ISOLATION

In part 2, chapter 1, after being summoned to the police station, Raskolnikov vacillates between feelings of defiance and the desire to confess. Relieved to learn that he has been summoned for debts to his landlady, he shares his Petersburg past with the "fiery" police lieutenant Ilya Petrovich, confessing that he had become indebted while engaged to his landlady's deceased daughter. Following this confessional closeness to Ilya Petrovich, Raskolnikov experiences an anguished estrangement from everyone and everything: "A gloomy **sensation** of tormenting, endless isolation and alienation suddenly made itself conscious in his soul" (emphasis mine; part 2, chapter 1). The narrator identifies the greatest source of Raskolnikov's suffering: "And what was most tormenting of all was that it was more of a **sensation** than a consciousness, than an understanding; an unmediated **sensation**, the most tormenting **sensation** of any **sensation** that he had experienced in his entire life" (emphasis mine; chapter 1). The quadruply repeated word "sensation"—part of Dostoevsky's critique of positivist science—underscores Raskolnikov's reliance on rationality: this "sensation" torments him precisely because it is not rational and therefore not under his control. Overwhelmed, Raskolnikov passively signs the document before him and actively conceives the "strange idea" to confess his crime. Yet he faints upon hearing the policemen talking about the murderer's escape.

In part 2, chapter 2, Raskolnikov refuses alms on the Nikolaevsky Bridge, thereby illustrating the dynamics of giving and receiving. After Raskolnikov is whipped by a coachman to keep him from being trampled, a merchant woman and her daughter take pity and give him a twenty-kopeck piece "in the name of Christ!" By extending alms, these two female figures offer Raskolnikov a lifeline to positive moral emotions, a way back from the state of alienation he effected by murdering Alyona Ivanovna and Lizaveta. As Linda Ivanits notes, the rite of almsgiving "assumes divine participation in both giving and receiving," as it "represents a mutual exchange in charity in which the destitute person receives material sustenance and offers in return a prayer for the wellbeing of the benefactor."[11] Yet Raskolnikov throws the twenty-kopeck piece in the river and feels "that he had cut himself off from everyone and everything, as with a scissors" (chapter 2). By creating a plot parallel with Raskolnikov's earlier, involuntary alienation in the police station (chapter 1), Dostoevsky emphasizes the difference—this time his alienation is self-willed. Raskolnikov's rejection of alms also recapitulates his recent acceptance and rejection of Razumikhin's charity. Moreover, it recalls his spontaneous pity and charity toward the Marmeladovs (part 1, chapter 2) and the molested girl (part 1, chapter 4), as well as his repudiation of it. Raskolnikov, it turns out, can neither accept charity nor extend it without regret. He seems to regard charity as a threat to his autonomy.

MORE DOUBLING

Razumikhin serves as a quasi-double of Raskolnikov: both are perceptive and intelligent ex-university students. Yet Razumikhin supports himself by translating, whereas Raskolnikov has stopped giving lessons. Here Dostoevsky subtly polemicizes with the popular theory that environment causes people to commit crimes. Razumikhin is equally poor, yet he does not isolate himself and develop a theory to justify killing and stealing. Moreover, he works hard to change his situation slowly rather than overnight. In short, faced with the same physical hardships, Razumikhin makes different choices. In part 2, he not only tracks down his university friend Raskolnikov, he also oversees his recovery. Furthermore, Razumikhin actively involves others in the recovery, including Raskolnikov's landlady, her servant Nastasya, and his own friend Zosimov, the medical student. On this view, Razumikhin serves as an important model of alternative choices. From Corrigan's perspective, however, Razumikhin's actions may be read as a way to manipulate his friend Raskolnikov.[12]

MORAL ILLNESS: UTILITARIANISM AND WHY READERS HATE LUZHIN

In part 2, chapter 5, while Razumikhin and Zosimov discuss the case against Mikolka the painter, Dunya's prospective husband Luzhin arrives. In this

---

11 Linda Ivanits, *Dostoevsky and the Russian People* (Cambridge: Cambridge University Press, 2008), 70.

12 Corrigan, *Dostoevsky and the Riddle of the Self*, 25–28.

noteworthy scene, Luzhin establishes himself as the novel's most despicable character by espousing the popular theory of rational egoism or utilitarian calculus, which is one of the novel's major polemical targets. In his oversimplified explanation of it, Luzhin argues that individuals acting in their own interest benefit society: "But science says: Love yourself before all, because everything in the world is based on self-interest. ... It follows that by acquiring solely and exclusively for myself, I am thereby precisely acquiring for everyone, as it were, and working so that my neighbor will have something more than a torn caftan, not from private, isolated generosities as now, but as a result of universal prosperity." Behind this utilitarian theory lies a belief that rationalism (science) can solve all human problems, as people acting in their own best interest will benefit those around them. Students may recognize Luzhin's theory as a form of trickle-down economics—if people at the top prosper, people at the bottom benefit. Dostoevsky's novel powerfully repudiates this argument—students need only remember Marmeladov's story of the rich man who did not pay his daughter Sonya either for her labor or for the material of the shirts she made him (part 1, chapter 2). In short, the wealthy man's self-interest robbed the poor woman of the means to support her family, pushing her toward prostitution. Given the poverty and suffering in this novel, Luzhin's utilitarian calculus seems particularly callous.

But Luzhin's worst crime in Dostoevsky's view may be his distortion of Christ's message. He alters Christ's command "to love others as you love yourself" (Matt. 22:39; Luke 3:10–11) and proclaims, "Science says, love yourself above all others." As Nina Perlina demonstrates, Dostoevsky uses the Bible as the ultimate authoritative text.[13] Luzhin's distortions of Christ's words reveal his egocentric, calculating nature and his willingness to use any means to obtain his own ends. Here Luzhin also denigrates the Christian charity of St. Martin of Tours, who cut his cloak in half and gave the other half to a beggar (Christ).

Dostoevsky does not let Luzhin's words or deeds speak for themselves, however. In full polemical mode, he has Razumikhin roundly denounce Luzhin's ideas as outdated and debased commonplaces. A few pages later, Raskolnikov refutes Luzhin's ideas by exposing the potential effects of his theory: "Get to the consequences of what you have been preaching, and it will turn out that you can go around putting a knife in people." Do we appreciate the irony of Raskolnikov claiming that utilitarian calculations can be fatal for others? That

---

13 Nina Perlina, *Varieties of Poetic Utterance: Quotation in "The Brothers Karamazov"* (Lanham, MD: University Press of America 1985), 11–29.

applied self-interest can lead a person to view others not as ends in themselves but as means to an end? Raskolnikov's argument actually exposes the moral implications of his own theory! The clue that Dostoevsky planted in part 1 is now bearing fruit. Before committing the murders, Raskolnikov remembers an overheard tavern discussion about whether it is acceptable to kill one person and use their money for the benefit of others (part 1, chapter 6): "One death, and a hundred lives in exchange — why, it's simple arithmetic!" The student in the tavern voices it; Luzhin amplifies it; Raskolnikov acts on it. Like his protagonist, Dostoevsky takes this idea and pushes it to its limit.

In reviewing this scene, readers may notice that the nihilist ideas undergirding Raskolnikov's actions are tavern commonplaces. Moreover, Raskolnikov himself is a cliché—a young man from the provinces who comes to the big city, squanders his family's money, and lives at others' expense. Raskolnikov's confession to the police of his debt to his landlady (part 2, chapter 1) confirms his mother's account of his family's sacrifices to support him (part 1, chapter 3). By the end of this remembered tavern scene, when Raskolnikov realizes that the ideas he heard in the tavern are *exactly the same ideas* as his own (part 1, chapter 6), we see how Dostoevsky has undercut his protagonist's seeming originality. Raskolnikov may be obsessed with uttering a "new word" (part 1, chapter 1), but his own idea echoes ideas in the air.

MORAL ILLNESS: NIHILISM

Like other nihilistic youth of the 1860s, the student in the tavern (part 1, chapter 6), rejects the status quo and espouses a belief that human reason can solve all problems. The student's belief that nature must be guided and corrected, otherwise "one would drown in prejudices" and "there wouldn't even be a single great man," reveals an inconsistency in his thinking (and Raskolnikov's). Belief in a "great man" is an oddly Romantic concept for a young nihilist. The word "prejudices," like the word "superstitions," was nihilistic shorthand for religious, moral, and aesthetic beliefs. So readers are puzzled that Raskolnikov, who prizes his rational faculties, is unaccountably superstitious:

> Raskolnikov was deeply disturbed. Of course, these were the most ordinary and most common youthful conversations and thoughts, heard more than once, only in different forms and on different themes. But why exactly did he come to overhear exactly this conversation and these thoughts now, when in his own head had just been born ... *exactly the same thoughts?*

> And why now, when he had just begun to carry the germ of his idea away from the old woman's, had he stumbled on this conversation about the old woman? . . This coincidence always seemed strange to him. This insignificant, tavern conversation had an extraordinary influence on him in the further development of the matter: as though it were actually some kind of fore-ordination, an edict. (Part 1, chapter 6)

This passage not only reveals Raskolnikov's unoriginality but his self-division. Readers must wonder whether his susceptibility to superstition comes from his head, his heart, or from an unknown factor. Raskolnikov's unconscious dream of the mare (his heart) initially saves him from his conscious daydream of murder (his head), but when he overhears that Lizaveta will be away the next evening, he feels "like a man condemned to death. He did not reason about anything, he was quite incapable of reasoning, but he felt with his whole being that his mind and will were no longer free, and that everything was suddenly definitively decided" (part 1, chapter 5). On the day of the murder Raskolnikov goes into mechanical mode—"It was as if part of his clothing had been caught in the wheel of a machine and he was being dragged into it" (part 1, chapter 6). Whence this loss of will? Is Dostoevsky creating a link between death and mechanics?[14] Is he showing how the theory that Raskolnikov develops to dominate others deprives him of agency? Is he debunking the supremacy of rational thought? Is Raskolnikov's superstitiousness a polemical jab at Dostoevsky's nihilist opponents?[15] The only certainty seems to be that nihilism is a form of moral illness.

INDECISION: CONFESSION, ESCAPE, OR SUICIDE?

Raskolnikov's theory allows the extraordinary person to act immorally, but his conscience does not. Raskolnikov commits murder partly to prove his own superiority, but his desire to confess (punishment from outside) and his temptation to commit suicide (punishment from inside) suggest that his inner moral compass remains very much alive. In part 1, a very anxious Raskolnikov hears Marmeladov's grandiloquent confession. In part 2, chapter 6, a very ill Raskolnikov escapes Razumikhin's watchful eye, enters a tavern, meets Zamyotov, the

---

14 Liza Knapp, *The Annihilation of Inertia: Dostoevsky and Metaphysics* (Evanston, IL: Northwestern University Press, 1996), 44–45.

15 Belknap, *Plots*, 119–20.

young police informant, and taunts him: "And what if it was I who killed the old woman and Lizaveta?" This first partial confession of Raskolnikov startles them both, and Raskolnikov realizes he's not yet ready to confess.

Raskolnikov's desire to escape detection sometimes takes the form of suicidal ideation, that is, thinking about suicide. In part 2, chapter 6, as Raskolnikov leaves the suggestively named Crystal Palace tavern,[16] he meets an angry Razumikhin, who nonetheless invites him to his housewarming that evening. Minutes later, fearing that Raskolnikov will drown himself, Razumikhin looks for him. Although Raskolnikov eludes Razumikhin, the narrator shows him standing on a bridge over the Ekaterininsky Canal staring into the water. His contemplated suicide is interrupted, however, when a young woman from the neighborhood, Afrosinyushka, throws herself into the canal (chapter 6). Raskolnikov next heads to the police station but finds himself at the pawnbroker's building. After visiting her newly painted apartment and ringing the bell three times, he goads others to bring him to the police station. As Raskolnikov contemplates self-surrender, he sees a commotion, discovers that a drunken Marmeladov has been trampled by a coachman's horse, and takes charge of the situation "as if it were a matter of his own father" (chapter 7). Helping the Marmeladovs energizes him, making him feel "like a condemned man reprieved." Raskolnikov moves from passive to active: he takes on the role of benefactor, "but in asking Polechka to pray for him, he acknowledges his own need," thereby ensuring a full giving-receiving exchange.[17] Once again Dostoevsky demonstrates the need for mutual giving.

Now full of resistance, Raskolnikov leaves, crossing the same bridge where he had earlier contemplated suicide, thinks "my life hasn't died with the old crone," and heads to Razumikhin's housewarming. After the medical student Zosimov gives Raskolnikov a sleeping draught, Razumikhin accompanies him home, dismissing Zosimov's suspicions that Raskolnikov is mad because he believes Raskolnikov's fake confession to Zamyotov demonstrates his friend's astuteness. Arriving at Raskolnikov's, they see a light in his room. Raskolnikov clearly expects the police. When he sees his mother and sister instead, he stands "like a dead man" before fainting. Clearly, this is not the reaction readers expect.

Throughout part 2, Raskolnikov vacillates between remembering and forgetting, acknowledging his guilt and denying it. Most saliently, he feels a need

---

16 Sarah J. Young, "The Crystal Palace," in Martinsen and Maiorova, *Dostoevsky in Context*, 176–84.

17 Ivanits, *Dostoevsky and the Russian People*, 73.

to end his indecision and identifies two possibilities—confession or suicide. Diverted from suicide by disgust at Afrosinyushka's failed attempt, he moves toward confession. He not only heads toward the police station, but also taunts others to take him there. His moments of weakness alternate with moments of strength—seeing an attempted suicide removes that desire; helping the Marmeladovs restores his sense of agency. Ironically, giving the Marmeladovs most of his money increases the debt he owes his mother and sister. Raskolnikov asks Polechka to pray for him, then revels in his sense of power (chapter 7). Yet when his mother and sister throw themselves at him, "he stood like one dead" (chapter 7). Consciousness and unconsciousness, power and weakness, life and death. Readers reel with Raskolnikov. And Dostoevsky's contemporaries have to wait another month for the next serial installment.

CHAPTER 4

Parts 3 to 5: In and Out of Raskolnikov's Mind

PART 3: RASKOLNIKOV FROM THE OUTSIDE

Like part 2, part 3 begins and ends in Raskolnikov's cramped room; it also keeps readers' attention focused on him. Yet Dostoevsky finally affords readers our first extended stretches outside Raskolnikov's fevered brain by providing other characters' perspectives on him: Razumikhin (chapter 2), the young medical student Zosimov (chapter 3), Raskolnikov's sister Dunya (chapter 3), and the judicial investigator Porfiry Petrovich (chapter 5). By ending with Raskolnikov's second unconscious dream, part 3 plunges us back into his psyche.

THE OBSERVERS: RAZUMIKHIN, ZOSIMOV, DUNYA, SONYA

In part 3, readers get a better sense of Razumikhin's importance for the novel. In chapter 1, Razumikhin keeps the themes of rational calculation, suicide, and mental illness alive by condemning Luzhin's stinginess, persuading Pulcheria Alexandrovna to leave her son's room by hinting at Raskolnikov's susceptibility to suicide, and confiding Zosimov's fears that Raskolnikov may be touched by madness. Zosimov reassures Pulcheria and Dunya that his patient is sleeping and diagnoses a moral as well as physical origin to Raskolnikov's illness. When Zosimov observes Razumikhin's attraction to Dunya and calls it a "daydream" (chapter 1), Dostoevsky subtly contrasts the two friends: Razumikhin daydreams of love, Raskolnikov of murder. While Raskolnikov pushes his family away, Razumikhin yearns to join them. We now see that Razumikhin serves as partial double for Raskolnikov: both are poor, generous, former university students, who love their families. Yet Razumikhin works hard, brings people together, and daydreams of love, while Raskolnikov has stopped working, isolates himself, and daydreams of murder. Both men seem spontaneously generous, yet readers may wonder whether Razumikhin is more a meddler than a generous friend.[1]

In chapter 2, Razumikhin offers Raskolnikov's family a perspicuous analysis of his friend's divided self:

> I've known Rodion for a year and a half: sullen, gloomy, arrogant, and proud; recently (and maybe much earlier) touchy and hypochondriacal.[2] Magnanimous and kind. He doesn't express his feelings and would rather commit a cruelty than express his heart with words. At times, however, he's not hypochondriacal at all, just inhumanly cold and unfeeling, exactly as though there were two opposing characters in him, changing places with one another. (Part 3, chapter 2)

Since Razumikhin's analysis confirms readers' observations, we generally view him as a reliable observer.

When Raskolnikov awakens in chapter 3, the narrator focuses on other characters' perceptions of him. First is Zosimov, who was "observing and studying his patient with all the youthful ardor of a doctor who has just begun to practice." Zosimov's professional observations highlight the disjunction between Raskolnikov's words and actions. Surprised that Raskolnikov seems to regard his family's arrival not as an occasion for joy but as an ordeal, Zosimov observes that "yesterday's monomaniac" is repressing his emotions. Dostoevsky's narrator then notes the gap between Zosimov's expectation that his family's arrival will have a healing effect on Raskolnikov and his observations that the ensuing conversation seems to open an old wound. Zosimov offers an astute diagnosis: "I do not know the underlying causes, but they must be well-known to you. You are an intelligent person and, of course, have observed yourself. It seems to me that the beginning of your disorder partially coincides with your leaving the university. You cannot remain without occupation" (chapter 3). By drawing

---

1 Corrigan, *Dostoevsky and the Riddle of the Self*, 25–28.
2 During the nineteenth century, hypochondria was defined as "a minor degree of melancholy, a disposition toward pensiveness, toward dark thoughts; *khandra* (depression)" (Vladimir Ivanovich Dal', *Tolkovyi slovar' zhivogo velikorusskogo iazyka*, 7th ed. [Moscow: M. O. Vol'f, 1880–82; repr., Moscow: Russkii iazyk, 1978–80], 1:351).

attention to Raskolnikov's self-chosen self-enclosure, Zosimov leads readers to wonder whether obsessive thinking might be the cause or effect of his choice.

Where Zosimov sees symptoms, Dunya sees playacting. When Razumikhin misinterprets Raskolnikov's teasing, the narrator remarks on what a difference family knowledge can make: "Had he [Razumikhin] been more penetrating, he would have seen that there was no sentimental disposition here, rather something quite opposite. But Avdotya Romanovna noticed it" (chapter 3). These observers allow Dostoevsky to model keen observation and teach us how to read his novel and its fictional characters. The verb I translate as "watch" is *sledit'*—to follow or investigate—a verb that is used for judicial as well as medical investigations. If we want to understand Raskolnikov, we must watch him closely. As we watch him through the eyes of other characters, we share their cognitive dissonances—that is, we experience moments when our prior knowledge or assumptions clash with our current observations.

In chapter 4, Dostoevsky elaborates the novel's doublings by creating another ligature between Sonya and Dunya, who both sacrifice themselves for their families. Although the narrator describes Sonya through Raskolnikov's eyes, she reveals her own observational skills when she exclaims, "You gave us everything you had!" (chapter 4). This statement both cements reader sympathy for Sonya and creates the foundation for Dunya's and Sonya's sisterhood.[3] This scene also establishes resemblances between brother and sister, and between Raskolnikov and Sonya. In chapter 2, Razumikhin had blurted out that Dunya "resembles" her brother "terribly much, in everything even!" Now their mother notes that Dunya and Raskolnikov are "both melancholic, both sullen and hot-tempered, both arrogant, and both magnanimous" (chapter 4). And, like Raskolnikov earlier, Sonya is so absorbed in thought while leaving Raskolnikov's room that she pays no heed to her surroundings or to the lengthily described "man of about fifty" who follows her (chapter 4). This is the readers' first glimpse of the unidentified, enigmatic, and eavesdropping Svidrigailov, Dunya's old pursuer. Dostoevsky is connecting the threads of his narrative.

---

3   See Anna Berman for a rich development of Dunya's and Sonya's sisterhood in her *Siblings in Tolstoy and Dostoevsky: The Path to Universal Brotherhood* (Evanston, IL: Northwestern University Press, 2015), 64–78.

PORFIRY PETROVICH, JUDICIAL INVESTIGATOR, AND RASKOLNIKOV'S ARTICLE "ON CRIME"

Chapter 5, which includes Raskolnikov's first visit to Porfiry and the discussion of Raskolnikov's article "On Crime," merits close attention. Unaware that his article has been published, Raskolnikov asks how Porfiry had identified him as its author, particularly since he had signed it with an initial, a common practice at the time. Here readers get their first sense of Porfiry as an investigator, or *sledovatel'*, which derives from the verb *sledit'*, used earlier of Dunya as observer (chapter 3). Throughout chapter 5, Dostoevsky emphasizes Porfiry's observational skills by having his narrator stay close to Raskolnikov, who watches Porfiry watching him. It is up to readers to decide whether Porfiry is a benign investigator or a manipulative bureaucrat.

As readers analyze Porfiry's cross-examination of Raskolnikov and the ensuing discussion, we get a sense of Raskolnikov's theory, but we must also attend to the questions it raises as well as to who focuses on its ethical issues. After articulating Raskolnikov's theory that crime is always accompanied by illness, Porfiry challenges him to elaborate his unwritten premise that extraordinary individuals are entitled to commit crimes. The narrator notes that "Raskolnikov smiled at this forced and deliberate distortion of his idea." Although he accepts the summary, Raskolnikov carves out an exception:

> I do not at all insist that extraordinary people absolutely must and are always obligated to do all sorts of excesses, as you say. ... I simply suggested that an "extraordinary" man has the right ... that is, not an official right, but has his own right, to permit his conscience to step over ... certain obstacles, and then only if the implementation of his idea (sometimes perhaps salutary for the whole of mankind) demands it. (Part 3, chapter 5)

Here readers may recognize the underlying Romantic commonplace that geniuses' contributions to society permit their excesses to be forgiven. Yet how are we to understand Raskolnikov's claim that his ideas—namely, that all the world's great lawgivers were criminals, who violated the old laws by creating new ones (a distortion of the Romantic view of geniuses as innovators), and who "did not stop at shedding blood either,"—were not new, but "printed and read a thousand times"? Do we accept Raskolnikov's argument that people are divided into two categories "according to a law of nature"? While we may identify the two categories—the ordinary, that is, a conservative and obedient majority, who preserve the status quo and reproduce, and the extraordinary, that is, those "who have the gift or talent of speaking a *new word* in their environment"—we may not recognize the nihilism behind the idea that extraordinary individuals often destroy the present in the name of the future as they "move the world and lead it toward a goal."

The language and ideas of Raskolnikov's article, which was published in a fictional newspaper, not only mark him as a nihilist, but also derive almost entirely from the *Russian Word*, the "thick" journal that was the major organ of the 1860s Russian radical critics.[4] During the discussion of Raskolnikov's article, Dostoevsky reworks the original to emphasize the concept of crime/transgression by word play—repeating the nouns *prestuplenie* (crime) and *prestupnik* (criminal), and deploying multiple verbs (*perestupit'*, *pereshagnut'*, *pereiti*) whose prefix *pere-* (over) and roots *stupit'/shag/idti* (to step) denote a literal stepping over or transgression. This also reflects Raskolnikov's view of his crime (*преступление*) "as a mere overstepping of bounds (*переступление*),"[5] that is, overstepping of arbitrarily established bounds.

Porfiry's cross-examination reveals the ideological concepts underpinning Raskolnikov's thinking. Readers will recognize the determinism in his evocation of the "laws of nature" or the evolutionary theory behind his concept of genius. When Raskolnikov asserts that ordinary individuals who imagine themselves extraordinary "never go far" because they punish themselves—"Such a law exists"—we must ask ourselves whether he considers himself subject to this "law." Raskolnikov calls upon scientific thinking to dismiss the idea that there could be many extraordinary people, arguing that divisions among people "must be quite correctly and precisely determined by some law of nature." He elaborates: "An enormous mass of people, of material, exists in the world only so that finally, through … some as yet mysterious process … it may bring forth one somewhat independent man in a thousand," one in ten thousand "with a broader independence," one in a hundred thousand "with a still broader independence," and "men of genius—one in millions; and great geniuses, the fulfillers of mankind—perhaps after the elapsing of many thousands of millions of people on earth." Dostoevsky hopes readers will sense the incongruity between Raskolnikov's Romantic enthusiasm for originality and his deterministic belief

---

4   Derek Offord, "*Crime and Punishment* and Contemporary Radical Thought," in *Fyodor Dostoevsky's "Crime and Punishment*," ed. Richard Peace (Oxford and New York: Oxford University Press, 2006), 119–47.

5   Marina Kostalevsky, *Dostoevsky and Soloviev: The Art of Integral Vision* (New Haven, CT: Yale University Press, 1997), 84.

that such individuals are produced by the laws of nature. Similarly, we are meant to sense the disjunction between his teleological belief that there is some undiscovered yet mysterious purpose in the world and his claim that geniuses are produced by evolution.

Porfiry identifies other ideological incongruities in Raskolnikov's thinking: his belief in the New Jerusalem, God, and the raising of Lazarus. Dostoevsky's contemporaries would have seen that Raskolnikov speaks the language of the 1860s nihilists yet espouses the beliefs of the 1840s Saint-Simonians—Christian socialists who interpreted the New Jerusalem as a future paradise on earth. Porfiry detects the incongruity in Raskolnikov's use of the abstract language of rights when speaking of the bloody act of murder. Despite Raskolnikov's moral rhetoric, his repeated use of the verb *rezat'*, which signifies an act of killing by cutting with a sharp blade, calls attention to the language of violence.[6] Only the most attentive readers will remember that Dunya has used this same verb (chapter 3) while defending her decision to marry Luzhin: "I have not killed [*zarezala*] anyone yet"—an intriguing link between the siblings.

Razumikhin focuses on the moral dimension of this conversation. Although Porfiry first links the concept of killing and the language of rights by asking whether there are many who "have the right to kill [*rezat'*] others," Razumikhin picks up Porfiry's phrase—"those to whom you've granted the right to kill [*rezat'-to*]." He thus underscores Raskolnikov's coupling of rights and violence yet notes that "what is indeed *original* in it all—and, to my horror, is really yours alone—is that you do still permit bloodshed *in all conscience* and, pardon me, even with such fanaticism." By using the phrase "*in all conscience*," Razumikhin stresses moral transgression, the stepping over of God-given law.[7] Razumikhin thus points out the hubris of Raskolnikov's theory and also shows us a way to read with great moral sensitivity.

More reductively, Zamyotov amplifies the scene's Napoleonic theme. Although Raskolnikov concedes that he may have regarded himself as extraordinary, he proclaims: "I do not consider myself a Muhammad or a Napoleon." The responses—Porfiry's "who in our Russia today does not consider himself to be a Napoleon?" and Zamyotov's "Wasn't it some future Napoleon who

---

6   Olga Meerson, *Dostoevsky's Taboos* (Dresden: Dresden University Press, 1998), 69–70.

7   See Vadim Shkolnikov on Dostoevsky's contribution to the history of conscientiousness/conscience. Vadim Shkolnikov, "Dostoevskii and the Birth of the Conscientious Terrorist: From the Underground Man to Underground Russia," *The Slavonic and East European Review* 99, no. 1 (January 2021): 124–54.

knocked off our Alyona Ivanovna with an axe last week?"—demonstrate the banality of considering oneself a Napoleon in 1860s Russia.[8]

PART 3, CHAPTER 6:
THE UNCONSCIOUS DREAM OF IMPOTENT KILLING

As Raskolnikov returns from Porfiry's, a tradesman outside his building accuses him of the murders. Since Raskolnikov wonders whether this encounter is real,[9] Dostoevsky generates epistemic uncertainty in readers, making us wonder whether Raskolnikov's conscience has begun to manifest itself externally.

Shaken by the encounter, Raskolnikov returns to his room and agonizes about his crime's insignificant nature: "Napoleon, pyramids, Waterloo—and a scraggy, repulsive registrar's widow, an old crone, a moneylender with a red trunk under her bed—so, how is someone like Porfiry Petrovich going to digest that! … It's not for them to digest!" Raskolnikov alternates between contempt for others and contempt for self. As he acknowledges his repressed self-knowledge, self-contempt triumphs: "That's why, that's why I am definitely a louse," he added, grinding his teeth, "because I am myself perhaps even more nasty and repulsive than the louse I killed, and I sensed beforehand that I would tell myself so after I killed her." Readers are expecting guilt, yet as Raskolnikov curses the old woman, he evinces none: "Oh, how I hate that little old crone now! If she recovered, I think I'd kill her again!" These are not the words of a repentant man. In fact, Raskolnikov next dreams that he is killing her again.

Raskolnikov's unconscious dream of impotent killing receives less critical attention than his unconscious dream of the mare, because it highlights his shame. Shame is emotionally difficult to witness—both in real life and on the page. This dream contains shame's essential components: exposure, painful self-consciousness, desire to flee, paralysis. The pain of shame aroused stems from a sense of being exposed that triggers a person's feelings of inferiority,

---

8   While Raskolnikov, Porfiry, and Zamyotov refer to the historical Napoleon, Dostoevsky may be reminding his contemporaries of Napoleon III's *Life of Julius Caesar*, a thinly veiled glorification of Napoleon I, which was very popular following its publication in 1865. Twenty-first-century readers may be unaware of Napoleon III's book, yet Dostoevsky's contemporaries would have known that it advocated for "the role and rights of 'extraordinary natures'" (Donald Fanger, "Apogee: *Crime and Punishment*," in Peace, *Fyodor Dostoevsky's Crime and Punishment*, 22). Cf. Gary Rosenshield's article: "*Crime and Punishment*, Napoleon, and the Great Man Theory," *Dostoevsky Studies* 23 (2020): 78–104.

9   Carol Apollonio, "On Devils and Doors: Raskolnikov's Ontological Problem," *Dostoevsky and World Culture* 1 (2019): 97.

inadequacy, defectiveness, or exclusion. After his encounter with the tradesman, a potential witness, Raskolnikov dreams that he repeatedly hits the old
crone on her head, directing his rage outward. When she doesn't stir, he bends
down, peeks at her face: "and went dead: the little old crone was sitting and
laughing—simply dissolving in soft, inaudible laughter." In Raskolnikov's
unconscious, the victim lives and laughs, and the murderer metaphorically dies.

The dream includes the standard responses to shame—flight and/or
paralysis. Hearing laughter and whispering from the bedroom, Raskolnikov
"hastened to run away, but the whole entryway was already full of people, the
doors to the stairs were wide open, and on the landing, on the stairway, and
farther down—there were people, head to head, all looking—but all lurking
and waiting, silent ... His heart contracted, his feet do not move, they have
become rooted ... He wanted to cry out—and woke up." As witnesses multiply,
Raskolnikov's sense of helplessness, mortification, fear, and immobility esca-
late. Like the dream of the mare, this dream reveals Raskolnikov's unconscious
fears. Instead of anticipating guilt, however, this dream exposes Raskolnikov's
shame. He must confront the crushing fact that he is not the extraordinary man
he wants to be. His crime did not fail literally, but figuratively: in killing two
women, he killed his dream of greatness.

In part 3, Dostoevsky starts moving readers out of Raskolnikov's head
by providing multiple perspectives on him. The discussion of his article "On
Crime" suggests that his desire to be extraordinary motivates a willingness to
dismiss morality in the service of ego. His encounter with the mysterious figure reveals Raskolnikov's fear of exposure. His unconscious dream of impotent
murder uncovers his sense of failure. As part 3 ends, Dostoevsky thus plunges
us back into Raskolnikov's head, and, fittingly, closes it with a cliff-hanger.
Awakening from his shame dream, Raskolnikov sees a mysterious guest, who
watches him and then "steps over" the threshold of his room. Svidrigailov has
arrived, but Dostoevsky's nineteenth-century audience had to wait two months,
until April 1866, for the story to resume.

PART 4: CRITICAL MEETINGS

Like parts 2 and 3, part 4 begins and ends in Raskolnikov's room, the cramped
space where he devised his murderous daydream. The literal center of the
novel, part 4 contains highly charged scenes—Svidrigailov's visit to Raskolnikov (chapter 1), Dunya's expulsion of Luzhin (chapter 2), Raskolnikov's first
visit to Sonya (chapter 4), his second visit to Porfiry (chapter 5), and Mikolka's

confession (chapter 6). While the meetings with Sonya and Porfiry deserve most attention, one should note that the mysterious appearances of Svidrigailov (chapter 1) and the man "from under the earth" (chapter 6) frame part 4, keeping readers tuned to Raskolnikov's fluctuating emotions and epistemic uncertainty.

PART 4: SVIDRIGAILOV—ANOTHER QUASI-DOUBLE?

The first three short paragraphs of part 4, chapter 1 highlight Svidrigailov's uncanny arrival and remind serial readers of the cliffhanging end of part 3 as Raskolnikov wonders—"Can this be the continuation of my dream?" Here readers may ask whether Svidrigailov is one of Raskolnikov's quasi-doubles. After all, both deny their guilt. Svidrigailov even does so by justifying his attraction to Dunya using the nihilists' catch-phrase "without prejudice"—"what is there in all this, in the thing itself, that is so particularly criminal on my part—I mean, judging soberly, and without prejudice?" Moreover, both Raskolnikov and Svidrigailov are dependent on women, as we see in Svidrigailov's story about his marriage with Marfa Petrovna.

Dostoevsky deliberately embeds biblical references, particularly ones related to the numbers three and seven, into Svidrigailov's story. Marfa Petrovna buys Svidrigailov out of debtor's prison for thirty thousand rubles then forgives his debt after he stays with her in the countryside for seven years. In the stories of Judas, who receives thirty pieces of silver for betraying Jesus after which he hangs himself (Matt. 26:15, 27:3–5), and Jacob, tricked twice by Laban into working seven years to marry his daughter Rebecca (Gen. 29), the numbers thirty and seven evoke the concepts of betrayal, suicide, bondage, and redemption. The raising of Lazarus is the seventh sign in John's Gospel and both this visit and Sonya's gospel reading may occur on the seventh day after the murder. Readers may note that both Svidrigailov and Raskolnikov are connected by their debts to women. We may also think of Sonya, who received thirty silver rubles for her virginity. As re-readers, we may recall Svidrigailov's announcement that Dunya will receive three thousand rubles from Marfa Petrovna. With these biblical references, Dostoevsky reinforces the novel's religious dimension. The fact that Marfa Petrovna can buy Svidrigailov out of prison for three thousand rubles and can leave three thousand rubles to Dunya provide another twist on the woman question: Russian women were legally advantaged over many of their European counterparts because they could own property in their own name.

Readers must also attend to the connections between Svidrigailov and Sonya: aside from being neighbors, they also share biblical associations and an interest in otherworldly matters.[10] As Svidrigailov confesses that he has seen Marfa Petrovna's ghost three times and that she enters and leaves through a locked door (part 4, chapter 1), Dostoevsky evokes Pushkin's short story "Queen of Spades" (1834), which helped establish the Russian literary tradition of the Petersburg text. A Petersburg text blurs the line between objective reality and the fantastic. It thus creates interpretive doubt and leaves readers uncertain whether the events described actually occurred or were produced by a character's increasingly unstable mind. In asserting that ghosts appear only to sick people, Svidrigailov identifies himself as a sick person. This links him to Raskolnikov, who questioned both the reality of the "man from under the earth" in part 3 and will soon question Svidrigailov's reality to Razumikhin (chapter 2): "just now it seemed to me that perhaps I really am mad and only saw a specter!" After Sonya confesses that she's seen her dead father (chapter 4), the three are linked. Dostoevsky thus prepares readers for part 6 when Raskolnikov identifies Sonya and Svidrigailov as his alternatives—confession or escape.

Svidrigailov is the novel's most enigmatic character: a former card sharp and seducer, he sees ghosts. He is reputedly responsible for three deaths—that of his wife, his former servant Filka, and Mme Resslich's teenage ward, whom he reportedly raped. Here we find another ligature to Raskolnikov, who may also be responsible for three deaths, particularly if Lizaveta was "constantly pregnant" as the student in the tavern claimed (part 1, chapter 6). Yet Svidrigailov also provides for the Marmeladov children, supplies Sonya with the three thousand rubles that allows her to follow Raskolnikov to Siberia, and gives his prospective bride a considerable dowry. Raskolnikov senses that Svidrigailov poses an ongoing threat to Dunya, yet his timely announcement of Marfa Petrovna's three-thousand-ruble legacy saves Dunya from Luzhin's calculating clutches. While Svidrigailov does some good,[11] he is haunted by the three deaths he is reputedly responsible for, another link to Raskolnikov. Moreover, Raskolnikov's dream of killing the pawnbroker and Svidrigailov's dream of the little girl are nightmarishly real and seem connected to a demonic

---

10 Knapp, *Annihilation of Inertia*, 57.

11 See Carol Apollonio, who points out that readers only hear about, but do not see, the evil Svidrigailov is accused of both by others and by himself: "A hard look at the text will yield only hearsay (gossip) evidence of Svidrigailov's criminal behavior." Apollonio, *Dostoevsky's Secrets* (Evanston, IL: Northwestern University Press, 2009), 75.

force, a potential reminder of Svidrigailov's vision of eternity as a spider-filled bathhouse—a Russian folkloric location considered the gathering place for evil spirits and the unclean dead.[12]

PART 4: LUZHIN—THE REAL VILLAIN?

Part 4, chapter 2 opens with Raskolnikov's epistemic uncertainty about Svidrigailov's recent visit and ends as Dunya breaks with Luzhin. Readers have been waiting for a showdown between brother and fiancé ever since Raskolnikov received his mother's letter (part 1, chapter 3). Anticipation heightens in part 3, when Raskolnikov reads Luzhin's letter containing the ultimatum—your brother or me—which echoes Raskolnikov's earlier ultimatum—"either me or Luzhin" (part 3, chapter 3). Because of his nakedly professed self-interest, Luzhin's expulsion is one of the novel's most satisfying scenes. While readers remember the characterization of Luzhin in Pulcheria's letter, we should also attend to Raskolnikov's unexpected critique of Luzhin's letter (part 3, chapter 3). The fact that Luzhin writes like a bureaucrat demonstrates that he has no originality, no word of his own: he is a cog in the great Petrine machine.

As part 4, chapter 3 opens, the narrator reveals Luzhin's daydream of absolute power over the beautiful, highly educated, but impoverished Dunya, from whom he expects lifelong gratitude and adoration. This rare glimpse into another character's psyche establishes Luzhin as the novel's most despicable character. The fact that Dostoevsky uses the same word to designate Luzhin's daydream of domination, Raskolnikov's daydream of murder, and Razumikhin's daydream of love provides a study in moral contrast. Unfortunately for Luzhin, he is all calculation, one of the worst sins in Dostoevsky's moral universe (another being violence against innocent children).

As part 4, chapter 4 closes, the Raskolnikov women have liberated themselves from Luzhin and adopted Razumikhin's publishing project, giving them a reason to remain in Petersburg. As he leaves them, Raskolnikov confesses non-verbally to Razumikhin, the second of Raskolnikov's near confessions in the novel. The first was with Zamyotov in the Crystal Palace (part 2, chapter 6). Ahead lie his promise to tell Sonya who killed Lizaveta (part 4, chapter 4); his near confession to Porfiry (part 4, chapter 5); his "confession" to Sonya (part 5, chapter 4); his acknowledgment to Dunya (part 6, chapter 7); and his full confession to Ilya Petrovich at the police station (part 6, chapter 8). As this chapter

---

12   Ivanits, *Dostoevsky and the Russian People*, 51.

ends, Raskolnikov entrusts his family to his friend, who becomes their "son and brother," biblical reference intended (John 19:27).

PART 4: SONYA/SOPHIA—DIVINE INTERMEDIARY

Part 4, chapter 4—the novel's literal and figurative center—depicts Raskolnikov's first meeting with Sonya (diminutive of Sophia, a name derived from a Greek word meaning "wisdom") and her reading of the story of Lazarus (John 11). In the mystical theology of the Orthodox Church, Sophia is seen as an intermediary between the human and the divine. Furthermore, she is often portrayed as a Mother-of-God figure. Here we must keep in mind that during Dostoevsky's four years in a Siberian prison, he had only one book—a modern Russian translation of the New Testament—and imagine how well he knows this text. We must note how this reading scene unfolds. Raskolnikov, for example, vacillates between compassion and coldness. He shows concern for Sonya by criticizing Katerina Ivanovna, yet when Sonya responds with an "insatiable compassion" for her stepmother, Raskolnikov calculatedly torments her by saying that Katerina Ivanovna will die soon and Polechka will be forced to walk the streets. When Sonya cries out that God will not permit that to happen, Raskolnikov cold-heartedly poses the nihilists' question: "What if there is no God?"

Yet five minutes later, Raskolnikov falls to the floor, kisses Sonya's feet, and declares: "I did not bow to you, I bowed to all human suffering!" This is Raskolnikov's first bow, a critical sign of his eventual regeneration. Bowing indicates respect, the recognition of another's virtue. It is an act of humility (from *humus*, the earth), a lowering of self, thus a humbling of pride. In Russian culture, peasants kissed Damp Mother Earth, which they venerated as the source of life. With the advent of Christianity, Damp Mother Earth was partially assimilated into the cult of the Mother-of-God, revered as an intermediary between God and his people.[13] In Dostoevsky's 1860s journalistic writings, the Russian soil (*pochva*, in Russian) represents the common ground between Russia's largely illiterate, but Christian peasants, and the much smaller group of the educated classes.[14] In bowing to Sonya, Raskolnikov exalts yet personalizes her, addressing her familiarly (*ty*) rather than formally (*vy*).

---

13 Joanna Hubbs, *Mother Russia: The Feminine Myth in Russian Culture* (Bloomington: Indiana University Press, 1988), 57, 86.

14 Ellen Chances, "Dostoevsky's Journalism and Fiction," in Martinsen and Maiorova, *Dostoevsky in Context*, 273–75.

When Sonya declares herself a "great, great sinner!" Raskolnikov identifies with her as a divided self, asking: "How can such shame and such baseness mix in you with such opposite and holy feelings?" Raskolnikov posits three paths for her: (1) suicide; (2) madness; and (3) debauchery—all paths that seem more to represent his choices than hers. Raskolnikov is already associated with suicide and madness. Yet he posits debauchery, a descent into the sensual realm, as "the most likely" option for Sonya. Debauchery implies a loss of morality, which Dostoevsky links to loss of belief in God. Debauchery then seems more apposite for Svidrigailov, providing a link between Sonya and Svidrigailov in Raskolnikov's mind. In fact, Raskolnikov will accuse Svidrigailov of debauchery, and Svidrigailov will reply that Raskolnikov suffers from a similar disease of excess—"everything that goes beyond measure" (part 6, chapter 3). In short, the debauchery option seems to mark Raskolnikov's self-divisions: on the one hand, he is "young, abstract, and thus cruel," on the other, he believes in God (part 3, chapter 5).

When, like the nihilist he is, Raskolnikov questions Sonya's prayers, she exclaims: "What would I be without God?" Like a utilitarian, Raskolnikov replies, "What does God do for you?" In angrily claiming the moral high ground—"Be quiet! Don't ask! You are not worthy! He does all!"—Sonya essentially asserts that in order to know, you have to ask the right questions, and Raskolnikov is asking the wrong questions. In order to ask the right questions or make prayerful requests, one must have faith. At this point, Sonya sees no sign of faith in Raskolnikov, and Raskolnikov regards Sonya as a holy fool,[15] whose madness derives from her belief in God and miracles, a belief that clashes with her lived reality. Yet doesn't Raskolnikov's madness derive from the clash between his nihilistic thinking and his spontaneous feelings? This conflict of perspectives heightens the novel's religious dimension.

Just as we tread into atheistic territory, Raskolnikov sees Sonya's copy of the New Testament, learns that she got it from Lizaveta, labels Lizaveta and Sonya "holy fools," then presses Sonya to read him the story of Lazarus. In the remarkable scene that follows, Dostoevsky manages to ramp up the novel's dramatic intensity even as Sonya reads verbatim twenty-seven verses from the Gospel of John (11:1, 19–45).[16] This dialogue deserves a close reading both for

---

15 Harriet Murav, *Holy Foolishness: Dostoevsky's Novels & the Poetics of Cultural Critique* (Stanford, CA: Stanford University Press, 1992), 66–70.

16 The Gospel of John, Dostoevsky's favorite, greatly influenced the theology of Eastern Orthodoxy, which stresses the beauty, transfiguration, and resurrection of Christ. More influenced by the Epistles of Paul and the writings of St. Augustine, Western Christianity places more emphasis on the suffering and death of Jesus.

content and choreography. We may well ask why Dostoevsky chooses to omit the middle seventeen verses.[17] Does the scene enact a kind of Gospel rape—with Raskolnikov forcing Sonya to reveal her most cherished beliefs[18]—or does Sonya perform an act of radical Christian hospitality by sharing those beliefs?[19] Significantly, the dramatic story of Lazarus is found only in the fourth gospel, thereby reminding readers of number symbolism. This scene comes in part 4, chapter 4, the novel's center. Lazarus is raised on the fourth day. While Raskolnikov committed murder not four but seven days earlier, isn't he metaphorically dead? (Perhaps even three days farther gone than Lazarus.) In an earlier scene, Porfiry reminded Raskolnikov of the raising of Lazarus (part 3, chapter 5), thereby suggesting that Raskolnikov could be saved by his own beliefs. Here we may ask whether Dostoevsky's judicial investigator is a meta-physician planting the seeds of Raskolnikov's redemption or whether he is a professional willing to do whatever it takes to get a confession.

Dostoevsky closes the emotionally charged gospel reading with a sentence Nabokov hated: "The candle-end had long been burning out in the bent candle-holder, dimly lighting in this destitute room the murderer and the harlot strangely come together over the reading of the eternal book."[20] We may ask here whether this iconic description, which includes the novel's only direct reference to Sonya as a prostitute, deserves Nabokov's scorn.

The most disturbing part of this scene may well be Raskolnikov's identification with Sonya. He claims, "We are condemned together, together we will go," and asks, "Haven't you done the same? You also stepped over ... were able to step over. You laid hands on yourself, you destroyed a life—your own (it's all the same!). ... [Y]ou cannot hold out, if you remain alone, you will lose your mind, like I did." Raskolnikov identifies them both as transgressors who are going mad, yet he deliberately killed the pawnbroker in the name of a theory, whereas Sonya sold herself to help her loved ones. They may both be divided selves, but it is clearly unfair to equate their transgressions.

---

17 Ilya Kliger, "Teaching *Crime and Punishment*" (lecture presented to the Literature Humanities faculty, Columbia University, New York, April 2018).

18 Eric Naiman, "Gospel Rape," *Dostoevsky Studies* 22 (2018): 11–40.

19 Valentina Izmirlieva, "Hosting the Divine Logos: Radical Hospitality and Dostoevsky's *Crime and Punishment*," in *The Routledge Companion to Literature and Religion*, ed. Mark Knight (London: Routledge, 2016), 277–88.

20 Vladimir Nabokov, *Lectures on Russian Literature* (New York: Harcourt Brace Jovanovich, 1981), 110.

As this scene ends, we find another instance when Raskolnikov derives strength from those weaker than he. When a weeping Sonya asks him what is to be done,[21] Raskolnikov reasserts his nihilistic, Napoleonic theory: "What is to be done? Destroy what needs to be destroyed, once and for all, and not only— to take the suffering upon ourselves! What? You don't understand? Later you'll understand ... Freedom and power, most importantly power! Over all the trembling creatures and over the whole anthill!.. That's the goal!" Raskolnikov feels strong when he privileges his intellect. At those times he is bolstering his self-image, seeing himself as superior, a "lawgiver," a Napoleon. By weaponizing his words, Raskolnikov can thereby deny his feelings of weakness and bolster his sense of self as "extraordinary."

Dostoevsky closes this dramatic scene with the eerie image of an eaves-dropping Svidrigailov. This eavesdropping scene recalls other overheard conversations: Raskolnikov overhearing first the student and the officer, then Lizaveta and the merchant couple (part 1, chapter 6); Svidrigailov overhearing Raskolnikov's name and following Sonya (part 3, chapter 4); Svidrigailov eavesdropping on a conversation in the hotel on his last night (part 6, chapter 6). The act of eavesdropping links Raskolnikov and Svidrigailov, but this instance is particularly unsettling because Svidrigailov clearly enjoys it.

PART 4: WHY SONYA THEN PORFIRY?

Part 4, chapter 5, which features Raskolnikov's tense second visit to Porfiry, keeps readers focused on Raskolnikov's mental and emotional state. In this confrontation, Porfiry clearly wants Raskolnikov to stay, while Raskolnikov clearly wants to leave. Dostoevsky draws attention to the novel's construction by having Raskolnikov draw attention to Porfiry's investigatory tactic of talking about something unimportant and then "stunning" the suspect with a "fatal and dangerous question." Dostoevsky also embeds a meta-reference to his own novel in Porfiry's observation that investigation is a "free art" which should not be constricted by forms, as every crime, once committed, becomes its own unique case.

Note how Porfiry's double-speak (making generalizations while referring to Raskolnikov's case) affects Raskolnikov. On the one hand, Porfiry reassures Raskolnikov of his good intentions, cautions him to take care of his illness, and

---

21 *What Is to be Done?* is the title of Nikolai Chernyshevsky's 1863 novel, which became the bible of radical youth.

advises him to think of his family. On the other, Porfiry taunts him—redeploying Raskolnikov's image of distracting his suspect and "suddenly, like an axe on the head (to use your expression) stunning you." Porfiry's alternation between sympathy and accusation inflames Raskolnikov's anger.

Significantly, Dostoevsky has Porfiry pick up on Marmeladov's "nowhere to go" theme (part 1, chapter 2). "Where could he [the murderer] run away, he-he?" asks Porfiry. "Psychologically he will not run away, he-he!" Here Porfiry's use of the language of determinism seem ironic. First he declares, "By the law of nature he will not run away from me, even if he had somewhere to run away to." Next Porfiry compares his suspect to a moth before a flame and concludes that if he prepares some definitive ($2 \times 2 = 4$) evidence, his suspect will circle him and then "fly right into my mouth!" Porfiry's taunting seems to achieve its goal when Raskolnikov explodes and accuses Porfiry of suspecting him of murdering "the old woman and her sister Lizaveta." Note Raskolnikov's rare mention of Lizaveta; is this the effect of his meeting with Sonya? Raskolnikov's anger seems triggered by shame issues. First he shouts, "If you believe you have the right to investigate me legally, then investigate me; to arrest, then arrest me. But I won't allow you to laugh in my face and torment me, I will not allow it!" Raskolnikov so fears mockery that he vehemently repeats the phrase "I will not allow it" five more times. In short, Raskolnikov is losing control as he professes to claim control. Score one for Porfiry.

Significantly, Porfiry asserts that Raskolnikov needs "air" and "water"—leitmotifs that operate literally and figuratively in the novel. Already in part 1, Raskolnikov leaves the mainland to get away from his cramped room and the crowded city. On the islands, he has semi-conscious dreams of a desert oasis, where he drinks cold, "miraculous-miraculous" water straight from the stream (part 1, chapter 6). His resurrection will take place in the open air on the bank of a Siberian river (Epilogue, part 2). Yet we must ask why both Porfiry (part 6, chapter 2) and Svidrigailov (part 6, chapter 1), an unlikely pair, repeatedly tell Raskolnikov that he needs air.[22] While their advice emphasizes Petersburg's unhealthy environment, Dostoevsky's repetition suggests a metaphorical, even biblical, meaning.

---

22 Richard J. Rosenthal, "Raskolnikov's Transgression and the Confusion between Destructiveness and Creativity," in *Do I Dare Disturb the Universe?: A Memorial to Wilfred R. Bion*, ed. James Grotstein (Beverly Hills, CA: Caesura Press, 1981), 229; Konstantin Klioutchkine, "The Rise of *Crime and Punishment* from the Air of the Media," 103, *Slavic Review* 61, no.1 (Spring 2002): 88–108.

PART 4: THE FALSE CONFESSANT

Part 4, chapter 5 ends unexpectedly with Mikolka's confession. Dostoevsky's narrator recounts the ensuing scene in chapter 6 retrospectively from Raskolnikov's perspective, thereby giving readers access to Raskolnikov's mind again. Significantly, the false confessant "Mikolka" is a schismatic, that is, "he comes from the *raskolniks*," which may account for his sense of guilt.

Mikolka's confession forces readers to think about guilt and responsibility, and the uncanny appearance of "yesterday's person" "from under the earth"[23] underscores the thematics of guilt as the unexpected guest bows and twice asks Raskolnikov's forgiveness. When Raskolnikov responds, "God will forgive," to the second request, Dostoevsky reminds readers that forgiveness can have both an interpersonal and a religious dimension. After confirming that he was Porfiry's "surprise," the guest repeats his request for Raskolnikov's forgiveness, thereby stressing their interpersonal interaction. When Raskolnikov responds, "God will forgive," he acknowledges the incommensurability of human and divine justice. Yet, as the scene ends, Raskolnikov buries his latent guilt, reverts to his combative stance and, in a reversal, repeats Porfiry's words, "Everything's double-ended, now everything's double-ended." Given a reprieve, Raskolnikov takes up his sword again. The verbal skirmish between him and Porfiry is not over yet. He is still a free man.

At the center of this story of crime and punishment, Dostoevsky amplifies the emotional intensity—Dunya is saved from the clutches of Luzhin, "the murderer and the harlot strangely come together over the reading of the eternal book," and Raskolnikov escapes Porfiry for the nonce. Raskolnikov vacillates wildly: he worries that he is seeing ghosts, that Sonya's holy foolishness is contagious, and that Porfiry has real evidence against him. He draws strength from others' perceived weakness. Raskolnikov starts part 4 epistemologically uncertain about the existence of Svidrigailov and the man "from under the earth" and ends ready to "do battle again." The confession of the man "from under the earth" gives Raskolnikov another chance to escape.

PART 5: SHIFTING FOCUS TO SONYA

Whereas the first four parts largely focus on Raskolnikov and his family drama, part 5 shifts focus to Sonya Marmeladov and her family drama. Chapters 1

---

23 Apollonio, "On Devils and Doors," 97.

and 2 build toward the scandal of Luzhin accusing Sonya of theft (chapter 3). This scandal precipitates a second in which an evicted Katerina Ivanovna takes her family onto the streets of Petersburg (chapter 5). Between the two, Dostoevsky places Raskolnikov's highly charged confession to Sonya (chapter 4). The scandals reflect the main action by keeping readers' attention focused on issues of social justice, passed-on shame, and "nowhere to go." Part 5, like part 3, ends with Svidrigailov's unexpected appearance, intensifying the mystery around him.

PART FIVE: CHAPTER ONE—THE SET UP

Since the narrator rarely enters other characters' heads, we must ask why he enters Luzhin's to describe his anger at Raskolnikov, Lebezyatnikov, the landlord of the apartment he's just renovated, the furniture people, and himself in part 5, chapter 1. Do we note Luzhin's fear of exposure? The 1860s was an era of investigatory literature, characterized by Robert Belknap as "uncensored, and often splendidly vicious, journalism."[24] Luzhin clearly worries whether "powerful, all-knowing, all-despising, and all-exposing circles" might "expose him if he undertook this or that, or would they not expose him? And if they would expose him, then what for, and what exactly was it that one got exposed for nowadays?" This fear partially explains why Luzhin stays with his former protégé Lebezyatnikov—he wants to keep his finger on the pulse of youth. The satirical conversation between Luzhin and Lebezyatnikov, who parodically oversimplifies the views of radical youth on issues such as utility, legal marriage, and the woman question, amplifies the novel's social justice themes. The setup for Luzhin's accusation against Sonya is particularly painful to read. On the pretext of arranging a fund for Katerina Ivanovna, Luzhin invites Sonya to the quarters he shares with Lebezyatnikov. There he overtly gives her ten rubles for the fund and covertly places a folded 100-ruble note in her pocket. The repeated emphasis on money in this scene sexualizes the interaction—Luzhin suggests a meeting later that evening—evidence of his desire to buy Sonya.[25]

In part 5, chapter 2, the narrator creates an expectation of scandal as he expatiates on Katerina Ivanovna's frivolous funeral dinner for Marmeladov. Having witnessed his first wife die of consumption, Dostoevsky is aware that Katerina Ivanovna's illness helps explain her paroxysms of pride and vanity.

---

24 Belknap, "Survey," 110.
25 Apollonio, *Dostoevsky's Secrets*, 86–92.

As Katerina Ivanovna vents to Raskolnikov all her pent-up anger and disappointment that the respectable renters targeted for her display of gentility had absented themselves from the feast, she blames the German landlady, Amalia Ivanovna, thereby diverting attention from the actual reason, Sonya's presence.

PART 5: CHAPTER 3—SCANDAL

Note how the scandal scene in part 5, chapter 3 amplifies the novel's social justice themes even as it seems to deflect from the novel's central action. Privileged man accuses defenseless woman of theft; impoverished but proud stepmother creates scene; entitled man threatens to press charges, withdraws threat, starts to leave, and is stopped by a younger man protesting the injustice. In declaring that Luzhin has deliberately framed Sonya, Lebezyatnikov exposes the *whodunit* behind this "crime," but his inept speculation about Luzhin's motives parodies in a minor key the novel's major question—the *whydunit* behind Raskolnikov's crimes. This scene asks us to consider the dynamics of scandal—readers may be puzzled by Raskolnikov standing silently on the sidelines so long. The scene ends in chaos—thereby reflecting the unexpectedness and disorientation entailed in shame and scandal.

In Dostoevsky's world, scandal not only moves personal crises into the public realm, but also involves the exposing of shame.[26] This scandal reveals one consequence of socio-economic inequity: the poor and the weak, especially women and children, are particularly vulnerable to abuses of power. Luzhin's accusation exposes the already vulnerable Sonya to further shame, while also threatening the Marmeladovs with greater hunger, further loss of dignity, and loss of shelter. Raskolnikov's exposé of Luzhin, in turn, reveals the dynamics of passed-on shame: privately shamed by Dunya's rejection, Luzhin publicly shames Sonya. By having Lebezyatnikov and Raskolnikov expose Luzhin, Dostoevsky genders the scene: poor women cannot defend themselves against male abuse, while even poor men can fight social injustice.

Raskolnikov's exposure of Luzhin underscores the connections between the Raskolnikovs and the Marmeladovs, while highlighting the novel's theme of shame and exposure. Luzhin fears political exposure and suffers social exposure; he leaves the room and the novel. Raskolnikov fears criminal exposure and seeks self-exposure; he heads to Sonya's room, where he will confess, thereby exposing himself to moral examination.

---

26 Martinsen, *Surprised by Shame*, 2.

PART 5—CONFESSION

Part 5, chapter 4 houses the scene that we traditionally refer to as Raskolnikov's "confession," but a close reading reveals that Raskolnikov never confesses verbally—only visually. The choreography and body language of this scene are thus worth spending time on. It's also worthwhile to ask how many explanations Raskolnikov offers for his crime and how Sonya responds to each.

The scene opens with Raskolnikov's compulsion to tell Sonya who killed Lizaveta. The narrator describes how his initial courage dissolves into a sense of powerlessness and terror as he feels

> that it was not only impossible not to tell her, but even to put off this minute, even temporarily, was impossible. He did not know why it was impossible; he only *felt* it, and the tormenting consciousness of his powerlessness before necessity almost crushed him. (Part 5, chapter 4)

Why create this sense of urgency? What has happened to Raskolnikov's sense of control after exposing Luzhin's *whydunit* or to his sense of power from having saved Sonya? To compensate for his emotional weakness, Raskolnikov addresses Sonya with the formal *vy*. He reminds her what could have happened without him and Lebezyatnikov. Moreover, he aggressively asks her who is more worthy to live—Luzhin or Katerina Ivanovna. Sonya recognizes the dynamic of passed-on shame from their first meeting (part 4, chapter 4): when Raskolnikov feels weak, he attacks someone weaker. Here she asks—"Why do you ask what cannot be asked? ... And who put me here as a judge to determine who is to live and who is not to live?" Sonya thus halts his attack by raising the issue of divine justice.

After a long silence, Raskolnikov changes his tone and again addresses Sonya familiarly as *ty*. He confesses that he had come to ask forgiveness, covers his face, and feels hatred. When he opens his eyes and sees love, his hatred disappears: "It was not that; he had mistaken one feeling for another. It only meant that *that* minute had come." Raskolnikov "mechanically" gets up and sits on her bed: "The sensation he experienced in this minute was terribly like the one he had had when he had stood behind the old woman, having already freed the axe from its loop, and felt that 'there was not another moment to lose.'" By reminding readers of the pawnbroker's murder, Dostoevsky draws attention to Raskolnikov's sense of powerlessness before something larger than himself.

In the delicate confessional dance that follows, Raskolnikov and Sonya draw together, separate, draw closer together, separate, and then bond. By attending so closely to their physical movements, the narrator focuses reader attention on the wordless confession. The nonverbal confession, in turn, pushes readers to think of how hard it is for Raskolnikov to accept his guilt. The focus on their physical movements stresses the psychological difficulty of confessing. After Raskolnikov "went mechanically and sat on her bed," Sonya joins him. He cannot speak; she feels terror. He feels powerless; she sees torment. He confesses by asking her to "Look carefully."

> As soon as he said this, a former, familiar sensation suddenly turned his soul to ice: he looked at her, and suddenly in her face he seemed to see the face of Lizaveta. He vividly recalled the expression on Lizaveta's face when he was approaching her with the axe, and she was backing away from him toward the wall, holding her hand out, with a completely childlike fear on her face, exactly like little children, when they suddenly begin to fear something, stare fixedly and uneasily at what frightens them, back away, and, holding out a little hand, are preparing to cry. Almost the same thing was now happening with Sonya: just as powerlessly, with the same fear, she looked at him for a time, then suddenly, holding out her left hand, lightly, hardly at all, she rested her fingers on his chest and slowly rose from the bed, backing farther and farther away from him, while looking at him more and more fixedly. Her terror suddenly communicated itself to him: the exact same fear showed on his face as well, and he began to look at her in exactly the same way, and even with almost the same *childlike* smile.
>
> "You've guessed?" he whispered at last.
>
> "Lord!" a terrible cry tore itself from her breast. (Part 5, chapter 4)

By replaying the lead-up to Lizaveta's murder (part 1, chapter 7) in this masterful scene, Dostoevsky links Sonya and Lizaveta. Mindful readers may remember that he makes the connection in part 3, chapter 6, before Raskolnikov's unconscious dream of impotent murder: "'Poor Lizaveta! Why did she have to turn up there! ... Strange, however, why do I almost never think of her, as though I had not killed her? .. Lizaveta! Sonya! Poor ones, meek ones, with meek eyes ... Dear ones! .. Why don't they cry? Why don't they moan? .. They give all ... they look meekly and gently ... Sonya, Sonya! Gentle Sonya!'"

Sonya and Lizaveta are both poor and meek; they help others while being exploited by an older woman, which make them particularly vulnerable to predatory men. But we might note that the pawnbroker's wealth and isolation also make her vulnerable. This confession can be seen as a partial undoing of the spiritual damage Raskolnikov inflicted on himself by committing the two murders, an example of Dostoevsky revealing his authorial hand.

The confessional choreography continues. Responding to Raskolnikov's silent confession, Sonya falls on the bed face down, gets up, seizes his hands, looks at him, sees "there was no hope; no doubt remained!" She jumps up, wrings her hands, walks halfway across the room, returns to the bed, sits beside him, then shudders, cries out, and throws herself down on her knees— perhaps anticipating the three times Raskolnikov will bow down near novel's end: to his mother (part 6, chapter 7), to the earth in Haymarket Square (part 6, chapter 8), and to Sonya (Epilogue, part 2). "What, what have you done to yourself!" she cries desperately, throwing herself on his neck and embracing him. He recoils, she sobs, and "A feeling long unfamiliar to him flooded his soul and softened it all at once. He did not resist: two tears rolled from his eyes and hung on his lashes." Raskolnikov's tears indicate an internal softening. Sonya's response clearly reaches the depth of his being, momentarily melting his ideological defenses. Yet after Raskolnikov asks Sonya not to leave him, and she promises to go to hard labor with him, Raskolnikov says maybe he does not want to go. Just as earlier with Polechka (part 2, chapter 7), Raskolnikov softens, asks for help, receives it, and then retreats into his hard shell.

By sharing his burden with Sonya, Raskolnikov receives her compassion. Sonya then asks Raskolnikov to reveal the *whydunit*, claiming that she will understand "*inside herself.*" As a moral agent, Sonya expects a guilt script, that is, she expects Raskolnikov to acknowledge his crime, voice repentance, and move toward expiation. But while Raskolnikov goes to Sonya because he feels the need to confess, a sign that his moral self is responding to his guilt,[27] he swiftly retreats from this uncomfortable emotion. In what follows, he provides a laundry list of his explanations—poverty, Napoleonic self-fashioning, nihilist ideology, social utility, spite, environment, originality, and power—all of which Sonya debunks.

Sonya dismisses the poverty motive by exclaiming: "And how is it, how is it that you could give away your last penny, and yet kill in order to rob!" Murder and robbery do not square with her experience of Raskolnikov as a moral agent. Later in this scene, Raskolnikov himself will use the example of Razumikhin to

27 Raskolnikov's need to confess may come from a sense of shame as well as guilt—he calls his crime both "unmonumental" (shameful) and "sinful" (an occasion for guilt).

dispel the argument from poverty. He acknowledges that he had other options: "There were lessons; I was being offered fifty kopecks. Razumikhin works!"

Raskolnikov proclaims his power script, declaring that he wanted to be a Napoleon, someone who can step over moral and civil law without a second thought. Yet hasn't Porfiry exposed Napoleon-emulation as a contemporary commonplace (part 3, chapter 5)? As a member of the working-class poor, Sonya does not read contemporary journals and is thus more resistant to such "ideas floating in the air" (see Introduction). She also resists Lebezyatnikov's attempts to "develop" her with new ideas such as joining a commune, and she has stopped borrowing books, such as George Lewes's *Physiology of Common Life*, from him (part 5, chapter 1). As a believer, Sonya does not understand Raskolnikov's desire to transgress moral limits without guilt because it does not make moral sense: "It would be better to tell me directly … without examples."

Sonya's resistance compels Raskolnikov to try again. He offers a nihilist's argument for social benefit and radical change: "Well … well, so I decided to take possession of the old woman's money and use it for my first years, without tormenting my mother, to support myself at the university, and for the first steps after the university, and to do it all sweepingly, radically, so as to set up a whole new career entirely and start out on a new, independent path …" Sonya rejects the utilitarian calculus that a murder committed in the present is justified by its future benefits: "Oh, that's not it, not it," Sonya exclaimed in anguish, "how can it be so … no, that's not it, not it!" Sonya cannot accept Raskolnikov's materialist, utilitarian explanation.

Raskolnikov next tries to justify his crime by depersonalizing his victim: "I only killed a louse, Sonya, a useless, nasty, pernicious louse." Raskolnikov not only deprives Alyona Ivanovna of a name, but also demonstrates his contempt by labeling her "louse," thereby placing himself above her. Sonya's passionate refusal to accept his equation—"A human being—a louse!"—reveals the moral flaw in his thinking. It may also jolt readers into recognizing that we have largely accepted Raskolnikov's view of Alyona Ivanovna as a social parasite.

Raskolnikov next combines an argument from spite with an environmental argument—that his room cramped his soul: "Precisely, I *turned spiteful* (it's a good phrase!). Then I hid in my corner like a spider. You were in my kennel, you saw it … And do you know, Sonya, low ceilings and cramped rooms cramp the soul and mind! Oh, how I hated that kennel! And yet I didn't want to leave it. I purposely didn't want to!" The argument from spite may evoke Dostoevsky's underground man, who also uses the adjective *zloi*, which I translate here as "spiteful," but which also means "evil." Activating the word's multiple meanings allows Dostoevsky to add a metaphysical dimension to both works. Like the underground man, who characterizes himself as "spiteful/evil," Raskolnikov invokes that negative moral emotion as a reason for withdrawing from the world. And Dostoevsky uses Raskolnikov's spiteful/evil withdrawal "like a spider" to evoke Svidrigailov's vision of the afterlife as a bathhouse with a spider in the corner (part 4, chapter 1), a charged image that suggests the banal evil in Svidrigailov's soul. Earlier, Raskolnikov's mother had called her son's room "a coffin," a preparation for the story of Lazarus and the theme of resurrection; here he calls it a "kennel" (*konura*). While the word "kennel" stresses his cramped quarters and voluntary self-enclosure, it also suggests his self-contempt. But Dostoevsky's larger polemical target is the theory of the environment proposed by the radical critics—that social ills result from inadequate social structures: change those structures, eliminate poverty, and people will change, causing crime to disappear. Dostoevsky, who championed moral responsibility, polemicized against this kind of thinking for his entire career.

Without pausing, Raskolnikov speaks ecstatically of power and originality, and Sonya realizes "that this gloomy catechism had become his faith and law":

> he who dares the most will be the rightest of all! ... power is given only to the one who dares to reach down and take it. ... And then a thought took shape in me, for the first time in my life, one that nobody had ever thought before me! Nobody! It suddenly came to me as bright as the sun: how is it that no man before now has dared or dares yet ... I ... wanted to *dare*, and I killed ... I just wanted to dare, Sonya, that's the whole reason! (Part 5, chapter 4)

Readers may note that the harder Raskolnikov strives to be original and powerful, the more powerless and unoriginal he becomes. Sonya responds to Raskolnikov's quest for originality by doubling down on the scene's religious dimension: "You deserted God, and God has stricken you, and given you over to the devil!"

Finally, Raskolnikov returns to the power script that would negate his shame script:

> I simply killed—killed for myself, for myself alone ... I wanted to find out then, and find out quickly, whether I was a louse like all the rest, or a human being? Would I be able to step over, or not! Would I dare to reach down and take, or not? Am I a trembling creature, or do I have the right ... (Part 5, chapter 4)

Here Raskolnikov not only conflates being human with being extraordinary, he reveals his contempt for "all the rest." Sonya responds as a moral agent: "To kill? The right to kill?" Sonya's moral horror and outrage at Raskolnikov's justifications and ecstatic rantings offer readers another view of Raskolnikov and his crimes. In this confessional scene, Dostoevsky moves us out of Raskolnikov's head and into Sonya's. We no longer want him to get away with murder, but instead to renounce this gloomy catechism and turn himself in.

Even as Raskolnikov's unconscious, moral self pushes him to confess to Sonya, his defensive, casuistic self protects him from feelings of guilt. When she tells him to accept the guilt script—"Accept suffering and redeem yourself by it," Raskolnikov refuses: "How am I guilty before them? Why should I go? What should I tell them? … They'll just laugh at me. … They won't understand a thing, Sonya, not a thing—and they are not worthy to understand." Raskolnikov denies his guilt by defending himself against shame: he projects blame outwards, accuses others of evil doing, and expresses contempt for them. His response also identifies a critical difference between guilt and shame. While guilt, as Sonya notes, allows for agency and expiation, shame entails a painful passivity.

The three methods of ridding the self of shame—denial/forgetting, laughter, and confession—all involve distancing the self from pain by pushing it out of consciousness or by changing position, viewing self from the witness perspective.[28] Raskolnikov both confesses and forgets. Although Raskolnikov proposes to tell Sonya who killed Lizaveta, he constantly forgets Lizaveta as he talks. Here one can see Dostoevsky's narrative strategy: since Raskolnikov primarily conceived the pawnbroker's murder as a means to prove his originality and superiority, the pawnbroker represents a shame script, a fantasy of power that denies his weakness. He represses thoughts of Lizaveta, because she represents a guilt script—the unintended consequences of his intended crime. Sonya keeps Lizaveta's memory alive by talking about her friend. Dostoevsky keeps her memory alive by having Sonya remind Raskolnikov of Lizaveta. Raskolnikov's identification of Sonya and Lizaveta with children emphasizes the heinousness of the crime and thus his guilt. By dividing the murders into a shame script (the pawnbroker) and a guilt script (Lizaveta), Dostoevsky prepares readers for the abrupt shift in Raskolnikov's behavior at novel's end, where he stops foregrounding his shame and, through the Sonya-Lizaveta connection, begins expiating his guilt.

---

28   Michael Lewis, *Shame: The Exposed Self* (New York: Free Press, 1992), 128.

After gaining the compassion of his female interlocutor, Raskolnikov once again feels a surge of strength. Thus revived, he resumes his defiant stance.

PART 5: DRAMATIC DOUBLINGS

In part 5, chapter 5, the dramatic confession scene ends as Lebezyatnikov arrives, announcing that Katerina Ivanovna has gone mad. After Sonya rushes out, Dostoevsky breaks the emotional intensity with a little grotesque humor. As Lebezyatnikov accompanies Raskolnikov, he offers a materialist explanation of madness, citing "the little knobs" on the brain during the final stages of consumption. However parodic, this scene foregrounds the novel's madness theme. It also contrasts Raskolnikov's suspected madness from monomania with Katerina Ivanovna's consumption-based madness. In chapter 1, Lebezyatnikov voiced an oversimplified version of contemporary radical beliefs on ideological issues. Here Lebezyatnikov voices the current rationalist belief that if you logically convince someone they have no reason to cry, they will stop—a position Dostoevsky finds ludicrous. Dostoevsky pushes the parody further by having Lebezyatnikov advocate a Parisian professor's theory that madness is an error of logic. The near-sighted ideologue Lebezyatnikov thus holds two contrary views of madness. Nonetheless, he defends Sonya from Luzhin's vicious attack.

Overcome by a sense of isolation, Raskolnikov excuses himself and returns to his room: "Never, never before had he felt himself so terribly lonely! Yes, he felt once again that he might indeed come to hate Sonya, and precisely now, when he had made her more miserable. Why had he gone to her to beg for her tears?" Once again we see that Raskolnikov finds connection a burden.[29] When Dunya unexpectedly arrives, he sees "this one had also come to him with love," reinforcing the Dunya-Sonya doubling. As she leaves, Raskolnikov feels a strong desire to confess and give her his hand, yet he fears to do so. He wanders around Petersburg, feeling the acute anguish that has accompanied him throughout the novel: "'Refrain from doing something stupid with these stupid, purely physical ailments that depend on some kind of setting sun! One could end up going not just to Sonya, but to Dunya!' he muttered hatefully." Clearly, Raskolnikov's encounters with Sonya and Dunya remind him of his publicly unconfessed guilt, which he seeks to forestall. By blaming physical

---

29 Amy D. Ronner, *Dostoevsky as Suicidologist: Self-Destruction and the Creative Process* (New York: Lexington Books, 2020), 89–149.

factors for his moral anguish, Raskolnikov prolongs the painful vacillations between his heart and mind.

The onset of the novel's second street scandal—the first being Marmeladov's fatal accident—interrupts Raskolnikov's moment of solitary reflection. Lebezyatnikov finds Raskolnikov on the street and tells him that Katerina Ivanovna has dragged her children outside and is making a scene. As they arrive, Sonya is vainly begging her to return home, but Katerina Ivanovna wants all of Petersburg to witness the spectacle of their poverty and abandonment. Raskolnikov tries to halt this humiliating scene by reminding Katerina Ivanovna of her idea to start a boarding house. Katerina laughs, coughs, and declares: "the daydream has passed!" She thus uses the same word—"daydream"—that Raskolnikov uses for his conscious plan to murder and rob, that the narrator uses of Luzhin's daydream of domination, and that Zosimov uses for Razumikhin's daydream of love. Dostoevsky makes these connections to show that most of us are daydreamers who fabricate fantasies to enhance our status in our own or others' eyes. He is also preparing us for Raskolnikov's upcoming self-exposure in a public place (part 6, chapter 8).

This heartbreaking street scandal ends as Katerina falls, coughs up blood, and is carried to Sonya's, where she lies delirious, declaring that there is no need for a priest as she has no sins. Note that this statement evokes Marmeladov's death scene and the concept of forgiveness (part 2, chapter 7), bringing the Marmeladov family drama full circle.

Katerina Ivanovna's dying words—"They have overdriven the nag [*kliacha*]! ... She's overstrai-ained"—not only convey the strain of caring for her impoverished family, but also recall Raskolnikov's first unconscious dream, which uses the same noun to describe the old mare (part 1, chapter 5). More puzzling, Raskolnikov notices Katerina Ivanovna's "certificate of merit" on her pillow—a reminder of her happy childhood (part 1, chapter 2). The certificate not only evokes Katerina's humanity as she lies dying but also Raskolnikov's capacity for compassion.

We must also ask about Svidrigailov's unexpected appearance at Katerina Ivanovna's deathbed. He again surfaces as benefactor, a plot mover, and a threat. He solves a plot issue by declaring that he will use the ten thousand he had intended for Dunya to settle the Marmeladov children. Yet when Raskolnikov asks his motive—raising the *whydunit* theme—Svidrigailov stuns Raskolnikov by quoting the very words he had spoken to Sonya the night before: "She wasn't a 'louse' ... like some old crone of a pawnbroker, was she? ... And if I don't help, then 'Polechka, for example, will follow, along the same path ...'" Svidrigailov's threat of blackmail is also an act of kindness—he lets Raskolnikov know that he knows. Furthermore, it reminds readers not only of Raskolnikov's utilitarian thinking, but also of the novel's themes: the extraordinary man theory, the woman question, and the Marmeladov question of where to go when there is nowhere to go. Moreover, by reporting that Raskolnikov is "barely breathing," Dostoevsky's narrator evokes the moments after the murders when Raskolnikov (along with most readers) waited with bated breath behind doors, hoping to get away (part 1, chapter 7). Dostoevsky ends the novel's August installment with Svidrigailov and his threat of blackmail, leaving readers to wait until November before learning what it means for Raskolnikov that two people now know his secret.

At this point we must again ask why the novel links Sonya and Svidrigailov. We learn of each of them from others in part 1. Each unexpectedly appears in part 3. In part 4, Svidrigailov visits Raskolnikov (chapter 1) before Raskolnikov visits Sonya (with Svidrigailov eavesdropping, chapter 4). In part 5, Svidrigailov eavesdrops on Raskolnikov's "confession" to Sonya (chapter 4) before offering his help to Sonya and the family after Katerina Ivanovna's death (chapter 5) and letting Raskolnikov know that he knows. As we have seen, Sonya recommends confession. Raskolnikov seems to think that Svidrigailov represents a non-confessional way out.

Part 5 continues Dostoevsky's project of moving readers out of Raskolnikov's head by focusing on the Marmeladov family and Sonya. His narrator sets up two scandals—one in the Marmeladov living space, the other on Petersburg's streets. Twice the narrator reveals how shame begets shame: first when Luzhin, shamed by his rejection, shames Sonya by accusing her of theft; second when Raskolnikov, shamed by his sense of powerlessness, shames Sonya by asking whether she earns money every day. This gendered parallel gives readers pause—humiliated men humiliating a woman. The parallel between the despicable Luzhin and our protagonist Raskolnikov strengthens the gendered dynamic, so we may speculate about how else Raskolnikov resembles Luzhin. Although Raskolnikov can explain Luzhin's motive for framing Sonya, he cannot satisfactorily explain his own motives for murder to Sonya. We thus see that it is easier for Raskolnikov to turn his analytic abilities on others than on himself. Dostoevsky is reflecting us back to ourselves.

Part 5 also illustrates how scandal begets scandal: Luzhin exposes Sonya, provoking Lebezyatnikov and Raskolnikov to expose Luzhin. These scandals cause Katerina Ivanovna to seek justice: she tries to shame Marmeladov's former boss into helping her, receives a humiliating public rebuff, and then drags her children onto the streets, publicly humiliating them. The first scandal leads to the second, and the second recalls the earlier Marmeladov public scandal (part 2, chapter 7): both Marmeladovs—first Semyon Zakharych, then Katerina Ivanovna—fall and bleed on the streets of Petersburg and are brought home to die. Dostoevsky takes private crises onto the public streets to dramatize social ills: there are no social institutions to protect the Russian Empire's poor. The parallels between the Marmeladov deaths may also remind us that Alyona Ivanovna and her half-sister Lizaveta bleed and die in a private space before becoming public news.

In part 5's carefully choreographed confession scene, Dostoevsky uses body language to establish a deep connection not only between Sonya and Raskolnikov but also between Sonya and Lizaveta. By having Sonya repeatedly reject Raskolnikov's explanations for the murders, Dostoevsky moves us further out of Raskolnikov's head. Like Sonya, readers see his thinking from an outsider perspective, so we, like her, understand that "this gloomy catechism had become his faith and law." In short, Dostoevsky is converting us—we are no longer swayed by Raskolnikov's earlier nihilistic, utilitarian thinking. Sonya reminds us of our moral emotions.

Finally, in part 5, Dostoevsky again reveals how grandiosity serves as a defense against narcissistic vulnerability. When Raskolnikov feels weak and vulnerable, he becomes aggressive. When he receives compassion, he revives. When Raskolnikov shares "his gloomy catechism" with Sonya, he falls back under its spell and resumes his defiant posture. Dostoevsky warns us of the power of words, even as he puts us under their spell.

CHAPTER 5

Part 6: Last Meetings and Epilogue

In part 6, as the novel draws to a close, Dostoevsky stages a series of farewell meetings. Razumikhin (chapter 1) and Porfiry (chapter 2) visit Raskolnikov; Dunya visits Svidrigailov (chapter 5) and Raskolnikov (chapter 7); and Raskolnikov visits Svidrigailov (chapters 3 and 4), his mother (chapter 7), Sonya (chapter 8), and the police station (chapter 8). Each scene resonates with an earlier scene or scenes, strengthening the authorial message and making it progressively more difficult for Raskolnikov to reverse direction. For example, Dostoevsky dramatizes the breakdown of Raskolnikov's theory-hardened shell in a series of heart-softening scenes: first when he meets his mother, sister, and Sonya, then when he bows and kisses the earth in the Haymarket (chapter 8). The bowing in these scenes demonstrates humility (from *humus*, earth), a humbling of self, an acknowledgment of something greater than self. These bows also recall Raskolnikov's first bow to Sonya (part 4, chapter 4, anticipate his last bow to her (epilogue, part 2), and dramatize his reconnection to the world around him. The final meetings also highlight the decision facing Raskolnikov since part 2—confess or escape?

PART 6: RASKOLNIKOV'S FIRST CHOICE: PORFIRY OR SVIDRIGAILOV?

Throughout part 6, Dostoevsky stages Raskolnikov's choice between confession and escape by creating unexpected connections between Porfiry, the judicial investigator, and Svidrigailov, the potential blackmailer. As chapter 1 ends, Raskolnikov decides to visit Svidrigailov, who "seems to be waiting for" him, thinks of Porfiry, also waiting for him, and "such hatred rose up from his weary heart that he might have killed either one of them: Porfiry or Svidrigailov." When Porfiry unexpectedly arrives, Raskolnikov wonders whether he might have been eavesdropping—Svidrigailov's specialty. Porfiry claims to understand Raskolnikov and likens him to a martyr (part 6, chapter 2); Svidrigailov claims to understand Dunya and likens her to a martyr (part 6, chapter 4). Porfiry tells Raskolnikov it will be "more advantageous" (*vygodnee*) to turn himself in, and Svidrigailov uses the antonym "disadvantageous" (*nevygodno*) to explain how others might view Raskolnikov's odd habit of talking to himself or standing motionless in the streets. Both Porfiry and Svidrigailov represent the threat of arrest, yet both also express concern for Raskolnikov and advise him to seek "air, air, air!" (part 4, chapter 5; part 6, chapter 2).

PORFIRY PETROVICH AND DOSTOEVSKY: INVESTIGATIVE/NARRATIVE STRATEGY

In part 6, chapter 2, Raskolnikov's third and final meeting with Porfiry, Dostoevsky draws on the emergent genre of detective stories to model keen observation for readers. Both fan and publisher of Edgar Allan Poe,[1] Dostoevsky plays with the form of the detective novel, stressing the *whydunit* over the *whodunit* in *Crime and Punishment*, a novel that exerted enormous influence on Russian detective fiction and helped establish Russians' initial preference for the *whydunit*.[2] By having Porfiry explain to Raskolnikov how he determined the *whodunit*, Dostoevsky shows how Porfiry's method creates a psychological profile that helps answer the novel's *whydunit*, a strategy that mirrors his own.

Porfiry's process is both evidentiary and intuitive. After enumerating the clues and incidents that led him to Raskolnikov, Porfiry emphatically concludes, "One thing leads to another, one thing leads to another, my dear Rodion Romanych!" (Note the familiar form of the patronymic "Romanovich.") Significantly, Porfiry prides himself on comprehending Raskolnikov's character: "you are too irritable"; "aggrieved but proud, domineering, impatient —especially

---

1   Today's readers might think of Conan Doyle as the inspiration for close detective work based on material evidence, but his Sherlock Holmes series was not published until the 1880s, after Dostoevsky's death.

2   Whitehead, *Poetics*, 101–21; Louise McReynolds, *Murder Most Russian: True Crime and Punishment in Late Imperial Russia* (Ithaca, NY: Cornell University Press, 2012), ch. 4.

impatient"; "daring, presumptuous, serious." Upon reading Raskolnikov's article, Porfiry declared it "absurd, fantastic, full of pride, the courage of despair," and he thought, "Well, for this man it won't end there!" Now Porfiry declares, "he killed, and yet he considers himself an honest man, despises people, walks around like a pale angel." Porfiry observes, "And so I waited for you, and look, what a godsend—you came!" He claims that he saw through Raskolnikov's laughter at Razumikhin at the start of their first meeting: "but if I hadn't been waiting for you in such a special way, I wouldn't have noticed anything in your laughter. That's what it means to be in the right frame of mind."

Porfiry's statement about "the right frame of mind" reveals Dostoevsky's authorial hand. Behind his characters' backs, Dostoevsky offers his readers an apt prescription for good reading/observing. Like other authors of detective stories, Dostoevsky makes readers co-investigators. Like Porfiry, readers must remember many conversations, details, characters, and incidents as we form our interpretation. Unlike a judicial investigator, however, we are reading a text, which means that the narrator provides all the evidence that Dostoevsky has selected and arranged to guide or mislead us. Like investigators, readers draw conclusions by piecing evidence together, but unlike investigators, we are reading a text that can simulate the randomness of evidence or the serendipity of intuition. Like Porfiry, we must learn how to "wait" "in a special way" for characters, especially Raskolnikov, to reveal their personalities.

The professionals in *Crime and Punishment* employ their powers of observation sympathetically. The medical student Zosimov offers a clinical analysis, focusing on diagnosis and treatment (part 3, chapter 3). He leaves the psychologizing to his patient. Porfiry, by contrast, offers an investigatory analysis that attends as closely to Raskolnikov's character and actions as to material evidence. He wants Raskolnikov to confess not only for the sake of the accused innocent Mikolka but for the sake of his own soul.

Porfiry understands the complexity of life and investigation. Since "this cursed psychology is double-ended" and all his evidence "can be explained in the opposite sense," he yearns for a "trace," something that will prove Raskolnikov's guilt. Upon hearing about Raskolnikov's visit to the pawnbroker's empty apartment, Porfiry has an epiphany that works like an emotion: instant judgment, physical response, mental evaluation.[3] His automatic, non-cognitive evaluation is followed by a physiological response: "And then, when I heard about those little bells, I even stopped dead, I even began shivering." Then he

---

3 Robinson, *Deeper Than Reason*, 59.

consciously evaluates his initial judgment: "'Now,' I thought, 'here's that little trace! This is it!'" Despite the final cognitive evaluation, Porfiry declares: "And I wasn't reasoning then, I simply didn't want to." This puzzling statement reveals Porfiry's own divided self and his decision to choose his intuitive, emotional self over his professional, rational self.

To make sure that readers understand the process, Dostoevsky has Porfiry explain it to Raskolnikov:

> No, my dear Rodion Romanych, there's no Mikolka here! Here's a fantastic, gloomy, modern case ... Here are bookish daydreams, sir, here is a heart irritated by theory; here is obviously a resolve on a first step, but ... He forgot to lock the door behind him, but killed, killed two people, according to a theory. He killed but was not able to take the money, and what he managed to grab, he piled under a stone. It wasn't enough to bear the torment of standing behind the door while the door was being forced and the bell was ringing,—no, he later goes to the empty apartment, in a half-delirium, to remember that bell, he needed to experience that spinal chill again ...

After using reason to collect and process evidence, Porfiry is in "the right frame of mind" to understand the bell's significance. Yet note that Porfiry develops his theory of motive from reading and then discussing Raskolnikov's article—which is what we do as readers.

In this scene, Porfiry articulates Dostoevsky's belief that Raskolnikov needs others. When Raskolnikov asks, "And what if I run away?" Porfiry asserts: "You won't. ... you no longer believe your own theory — what would you run away on? ... You'd run away, and come back on your own. *It's impossible for you to do without us.*" However much Raskolnikov pushes against the ties that bind him to his family and the human community, he needs others—as much for his sense of identity as for his salvation. Here Porfiry acts as a spiritual counselor. Like Sonya, he advises Raskolnikov to confess. Like Sonya, he uses his own intuition. Unlike Sonya, who keeps trying to understand the *whydunit*, Porfiry treats Raskolnikov as though they both know he is guilty (which drives Raskolnikov crazy). Unlike Sonya, who does not want to believe that Raskolnikov could commit such a heinous, seemingly unmotivated crime, Porfiry acts as a judicial professional and appeals to Raskolnikov's reason by revealing his own strategy. He also exerts his power to give Raskolnikov three days of freedom in hopes that he will turn himself in.

SVIDRIGAILOV

As part 6, chapter 3 opens, Raskolnikov speculates that, whereas "Sonya represented an implacable sentence," Svidrigailov might offer him "something *new*," perhaps a way out. When Raskolnikov aggressively threatens to kill him if he still has designs on Dunya, Svidrigailov admits that he came to Petersburg hoping that Raskolnikov would *"tell me a little something new,"* thereby creating an unexpected link between them. Furthermore, like Raskolnikov, who has confessed his crime to Sonya yet denies culpability (part 5, chapter 4), Svidrigailov declares: "Why is she so good looking? I'm not to blame!" The similarities pile up when Svidrigailov (part 1, chapter 4), like Raskolnikov (part 1, chapter 4), equates Dunya's engagement to Luzhin with prostitution. Moreover, Svidrigailov admits that if Dunya had said, "murder Marfa Petrovna and marry me," he would have, making readers wonder if he had.

Like Porfiry, Svidrigailov offers an outsider's perspective on Raskolnikov. After commenting on Raskolnikov talking to himself, he calls Petersburg a city of "half-crazy people" with "many gloomy, sharp, and strange influences on the soul of man," a place where "the people get drunk, educated youth without activity burn out in unrealizable dreams … and disfigure themselves with theories."[4] Dostoevsky thus tips his authorial hand by having both Svidrigailov and Porfiry point to Raskolnikov's theorizing as the major cause of his crime.

In part 6, chapter 4, as Svidrigailov tells his version of the Dunya story that Raskolnikov learned from his mother's letter (part 1, chapter 4), he establishes another connection between the Raskolnikov siblings. Svidrigailov admits that he attempted to resist Dunya's beauty but Marfa Petrovna's stories about him aroused Dunya's pity: "And when a girl's heart starts to feel pity, then, it goes without saying, it's very dangerous for her. She immediately wants 'to save,' and bring to reason, and resurrect, and … well, we all know what's possible to daydream in that vein." By using *namechtat'*, a verbal form of the noun *mechta* (daydream), Svidrigailov establishes an unexpected ligature between sister and brother—Raskolnikov daydreams of committing murder, whereas Dunya daydreams of saving a man's soul. Both siblings thus have a singularly unattractive other as the object of their daydreams—a greedy old crone and a lascivious pursuer.

4　Svidrigailov uses the word for unconscious dreams—*nesbytochnykh snakh.*

Finally, Svidrigailov repeatedly calls Raskolnikov a Schiller, that is, an idealist,[5] thereby allowing Dostoevsky to draw further attention to the split between Raskolnikov's youthful idealism and his attraction to a murderous theory. Here we might note that in his pre-exilic life Dostoevsky "had once consented to unleashing murder through revolution."[6] Even though his personal convictions changed, Dostoevsky's early membership in a secret society with revolutionary aims explains his deep understanding of the revolutionary psychology that motivates some of his characters, including Raskolnikov.

DUNYA—SVIDRIGAILOV

In part 6, chapter 5, as Raskolnikov feels disgust that he had expected something from Svidrigailov, that "lowly evil-doer, that voluptuous debaucher and scoundrel," the narrator describes a horrified Dunya looking at her brother on the bridge staring into the water. This moment echoes the earlier scene when he gazed into the canal (part 2, chapter 6), reminding readers that suicide offers an ever-present way out.

The choreography of the surprisingly gothic meeting between Dunya and Svidrigailov evokes that between Raskolnikov and Sonya in the confession scene, but with completely different outcomes. Whereas Sonya initially experiences horror, she then embraces Raskolnikov, expressing compassion for his suffering, while Dunya's revulsion at the attempted rape is clear from start to finish. Significantly, when trying to blackmail Dunya by citing Raskolnikov's explanations to Sonya, Svidrigailov adds "vanity and pride," concluding that Raskolnikov is suffering from shame at the thought that he could conceive a theory but not step over moral limits. The ensuing scene raises further questions about moral limits. Dunya unexpectedly reverts to the familiar *ty* when she commands Svidrigailov to open the door. To avoid rape after he refuses, Dunya fires a handgun twice—once unsuccessfully, once grazing Svidrigailov's forehead. Yet she cannot fire a third time. Svidrigailov misreads her throwing away the gun, but when she declares that she could never love him, he lets her escape: he does not step over that moral boundary. Dunya's rejection of

---

5   Friedrich Schiller was a German idealist poet, aesthetician, and dramatist who was a formative influence on Dostoevsky in his youth. For the remainder of his career, Dostoevsky used references to Schiller to indicate a character's idealism.

6   Joseph Frank, *Lectures on Dostoevsky*, ed. Marina Brodskaya and Marguerite Frank (Princeton, NJ: Princeton University Press, 2020), 8.

Svidrigailov not only triggers his suicide, but also contributes to the novel's portrayal of women's precarious situations in 1860s Russia.

SVIDRIGAILOV'S DARK NIGHT OF THE SOUL

While his narrator tracks Svidrigailov in part 6, chapter 6, Dostoevsky constantly reminds us of Raskolnikov. Svidrigailov not only visits Sonya and gives her 3,000 rubles, he also predicts that Raskolnikov has two paths before him—suicide or prison (Vladimirka is the transit point for Siberia). Like Raskolnikov earlier, Svidrigailov stands on a bridge contemplating the water. After checking into an old hotel,[7] Svidrigailov has a series of semi-conscious dreams (*grezy*),[8] which anticipate Raskolnikov's semi-conscious dreams in Siberia (Epilogue, part 2). Moreover, as his narrator reports Svidrigailov's semi-conscious dreams of the young girl in the coffin and the bedraggled, weeping five-year-old huddled under the staircase, Dostoevsky blurs the boundary between the real and the imagined. Just as readers had once been led to believe that Raskolnikov had heard Lieutenant Gunpowder beating his landlady (part 2, chapter 2), here we are led to believe that the child is real until Svidrigailov awakens. Finally, upon leaving the hotel, Svidrigailov seeks a bush on Petrovsky Island—the site of Raskolnikov's unconscious dream of the mare (part 1, chapter 5).

Svidrigailov enigmatically kills himself in front of a Jewish fireman wearing an Achilles helmet. Although Petersburg firemen wore such helmets, which were common throughout Europe,[9] Dostoevsky may be ironically invoking the Iliadic hero's choice of a short but glorious life over a long ordinary one. He also may have Svidrigailov call suicide "going to America" as a reference to the soulless materialism that characterized Dickens's portrait of America in *Martin Chuzzlewit*, a novel that influenced Dostoevsky's view of the United States. Svidrigailov has led a life of pleasure-seeking, of mostly but not exclusively carnal pleasures. He seems to fear boredom. He seems to believe that Dunya could save him, but, as the philosopher Jeffrie Murphy suggests, she

---

7   Dostoevsky names the hotel the Adrianopolis, thereby recalling the persecution of Christians.

8   The word *grezy* is plural and denotes daydreams or reveries. Since I translate *mechta* as "daydream," I translate *grezy* as "semi-conscious dreams." Svidrigailov will later call his semiconscious dreams "nightmares."

9   Donna Orwin, "Achilles in *Crime and Punishment*," in *Dostoevsky Beyond Dostoevsky: Science, Religion, Philosophy*, ed. Svetlana Evdokimova and Vladimir Golstein (Boston, MA: Academic Studies Press, 2016), 368.

might have been just another pleasure he would eventually tire of.[10] We will never know—Svidrigailov hoped that Raskolnikov would offer him something new; clearly he thought that Dunya would. Perhaps in telling Sonya that Raskolnikov has two options—suicide or prison—Svidrigailov was projecting his own real or existential options.[11]

Svidrigailov is not merely a melodramatic villain, but a man of contradictions. He provides for the Marmeladov children, Sonya, and his young "bride." He releases Dunya. His past haunts him—he sees the ghosts of his servant Filipp and his wife Marfa Petrovna and has semi-conscious dreams of the young girl he reportedly drove to suicide. Despite his professed amorality, Svidrigailov seems to have some "pangs of conscience," as Dunya calls them. But, unlike Raskolnikov, he has nothing to hold him to this earth.

RASKOLNIKOV'S RETURN TO COMMUNITY

In part 6, chapter 7, a rain-soaked Raskolnikov returns from his own dark night of the soul. He visits his mother, learns that she's been reading his article nonstop for three days, and briefly experiences the pride of a twenty-three-year-old author before a terrible anguish seizes his heart. After avowals of love between mother and son, Raskolnikov's mother predicts a great sorrow awaiting him, and Raskolnikov asks for her prayers. When Pulcheria blesses him, "It was as though all that terrible time softened his heart all at once. He fell before her, he kissed her feet, and the two, embracing, wept." Raskolnikov's return to family and community thus starts with his mother. The bowing scene evokes his first visit to Sonya (part 4, chapter 4) when he does the same, declaring, "I did not bow down to you, I bowed down to all human suffering." By yoking Sonya and Pulcheria, Dostoevsky is pulling out the religious stops—evoking the mother of God as intercessor and preparing for the convicts in Siberia to call Sonya "Little Mother."

Returning to his room, Raskolnikov finds Dunya, sees that she knows, and confesses that he had contemplated drowning himself to avoid the shame of surrender. It is interesting to compare the narrator's detailed account of Svidrigailov's last night with the telescoped account of Raskolnikov's. Both characters wander in the rain and stare into the river, yet they make different

---

10 Jeffrie Murphy, private correspondence, June 7, 2018.

11 If Svidrigailov was projecting his own options, he might be indirectly confessing to his wife Marfa's murder, making prison an option for him.

choices. Raskolnikov not only clings to life, but he also has spiritual help: Dunya and Sonya pray for him all night.

Raskolnikov asks Dunya's forgiveness, and she embraces him—another step toward his return to community. Yet when she states that his acceptance of suffering washes away half his crime, the old Raskolnikov reasserts himself: "Crime? What crime?" Raskolnikov declares that he is surrendering "from baseness" and "maybe the advantage that Porfiry proposed." Dunya voices our horror: "Brother, brother, what are you saying? You spilled blood!" Raskolnikov then repeats all of his discarded illusions, including the extraordinary man idea, until the suffering on Dunya's face causes him to stop. Requesting Dunya's forgiveness once again, Raskolnikov asks her to take care of their mother. Yet when he nihilistically declares that "now everything will be on a new footing, broken in two," Raskolnikov is overwhelmed by his old anguish. Reverting to his old rhetoric revives Raskolnikov's suffering—a reminder of how we get stuck in mental ruts, especially through intellectual pride.

Upon leaving his sister, Raskolnikov feels the weight of attachment: "I'm evil. Why do they love me if I'm not worthy? If only I were alone and no one loved me, and I never loved! None of this would have happened!" Raskolnikov thus harks back to the novel's beginning, when he receives his mother's letter and feels the burden of her love, a theme as vital as his search for a "new word." Moreover, Raskolnikov fears that his surrender to the police will be "by the book," and thus not original, a reminder to readers that Raskolnikov has been seeking his own "new word" since the novel's first page.

In part 6, chapter 8, Raskolnikov visits Sonya for a third time, arriving just as Sonya is convinced that he has killed himself. His appearance thus seems a resurrection, perhaps an undoing of his earlier spiritual death (part 2, chapter 7). When Sonya cries, he asks for her cross. When he jokes about taking the cross on himself, his heart contracts. Seeing that Sonya plans to accompany him, Raskolnikov announces he will go himself and absentmindedly leaves. Yet even as Raskolnikov walks away, he wonders whether he loves Sonya and calls himself a scoundrel for daring to hope, "to daydream like that for himself." This momentous admission marks another step on his road to community. Here Raskolnikov consciously considers replacing his daydream of murder with a daydream of love. Raskolnikov now thinks about sharing his life with another.[12]

---

12 Nancy Workman, "Bone of My Bone, Flesh of My Flesh: Love in *Crime and Punishment*," *Dostoevsky Studies* 18 (2014): 87–97.

As Raskolnikov looks avidly around him on his way to the police station, he takes another step on his return to community: whereas earlier Raskolnikov threw away the alms he is given by a mother and child (part 2, chapter 2), here he offers alms to a mother and child, who bless him. As a sign of his inner change, this time Raskolnikov has no second thoughts. In the middle of Haymarket Square, Raskolnikov remembers Sonya's exhortation that he go to the crossroads, bow to the people, and kiss the earth "because you sinned before her, and tell the whole world 'I am a murderer.'" He feels an inescapable anguish, but then "all at once, everything in him softened," he falls to the earth, bows and kisses it "with pleasure and happiness"—a gesture of repentance typical of the *raskolniki*/schismatics.[13] A passerby shouts, "he's drunk," but another offers an explanation: "He's going to Jerusalem, brothers, he's bidding farewell to his children, his motherland, he's bowing to the whole world, kissing the capital city St. Petersburg and its soil"—a reminder of Dostoevsky's doctrine of *pochvennichestvo* (an ideology of Russianness rooted in the soil) and Raskolnikov's professed belief in the new Jerusalem (part 3, chapter 5). Seeing Sonya, Raskolnikov's heart turns over, and he enters the police station. Each one of Raskolnikov's encounters with others thus eliminates an escape option, leaving him with nowhere to go.

One may speculate that Raskolnikov surrenders himself to Ilya Petrovich (Lieutenant Gunpowder) at the police station rather than to Porfiry in order to save face. Turning himself in to Porfiry might feel like defeat. When Raskolnikov hears about Svidrigailov's suicide, he leaves the police station—evoking the theme of "air" associated with both Svidrigailov and Porfiry. Raskolnikov's departure and return demonstrate how hard it is for him to confess: this is the only time he fully names and takes responsibility for his crime.

As the moment of surrender draws near, Raskolnikov is still seeking a way out of confessing and imprisonment. Raskolnikov's visit to Svidrigailov and his contemplation of suicide represent attempts to avoid responsibility for murder. His visit to his mother represents the start of his return to community. When he bows down and embraces his birth mother (chapter 7), embraces his sister (chapter 7), then bows down to the primordial mother earth (chapter 8) and Sonya (Epilogue, part 2), he demonstrates humility and signals his return to family, human community, and God. The heart softening in these scenes of union signifies a crumbling of the barriers he has

---

13 Joseph Frank, *Dostoevsky: A Writer in His Time* (Princeton, NJ: Princeton University Press, 2010), 505.

erected. In psychoanalytic terms, the softened heart represents a weakening of Raskolnikov's denials and defenses. In biblical terms, it represents an opening to God's word.

THE EPILOGUE

The Epilogue offers readers both challenge and opportunity. Since Dostoevsky not only switches narrative strategy but also provides a happy ending, readers have long wrestled with the question of whether the Epilogue is organic or artificial. By considering the novel's geographical and temporal shift, analyzing Raskolnikov's prison experiences and semi-conscious plague dreams, and examining his resurrection in love, we can appreciate Dostoevsky's choices and understand his message, whether or not we like his novel's ending.

A NEW NARRATIVE STRATEGY

Throughout the novel, Dostoevsky's narrator moves skillfully in and out of Raskolnikov's head—a strategy that not only imitates Raskolnikov's internal divisions but creates a similar division within readers. We *feel* sympathetically toward Raskolnikov, but we *see* him critically. In Epilogue, part 1, the narrator adopts an impersonal, omniscient style to summarize the events of the eighteen months following Raskolnikov's confession, thereby creating a distancing effect that mirrors both the novel's geographical shift from St. Petersburg's crowded spaces to Siberia's expanses and its psychological shift from inside to outside of Raskolnikov's head. Here we might read the narrator's description of Sonya's factual, non-editorializing letters as a meta-literary commentary on Dostoevsky's new narrative strategy.

In Epilogue, part 2, the narrator returns focus to Raskolnikov, noting that while his physical circumstances have changed, his spiritual state has not. Just as earlier, Raskolnikov remains isolated and indifferent to his environment: "His chains he did not even feel on himself." Just as earlier, Raskolnikov falls ill and has haunting dreams. Just as earlier, Raskolnikov experiences an emotional change and bows down to a symbolic female. Dostoevsky thus recapitulates major plot events but with two major differences. First, Raskolnikov's class status and self-enclosure create hostility among the largely peasant prison population: whereas the other prisoners trust and revere Sonya, they regard him distrustfully and suspect him of godlessness. Second and more importantly, instead of responding to his inner anguish by stepping over a moral law and committing a crime, Raskolnikov broods over his old life before experiencing a rebirth and stepping into a new life.

Significantly, the narrator's account of Raskolnikov in Epilogue, part 2, echoes that from Sonya's letters in Epilogue, part 1. Sonya observed that while Raskolnikov was initially indifferent to her visits, he became habituated to them and had experienced *toska* when she got ill and could not visit. In Dostoevsky's work, *toska*, which I translate as "anguish," generally signifies spiritual anguish and is often accompanied by a sense of spiritual oppression, social alienation, and vague longing. Moreover, like a dream term or a primal word, *toska* can embody its opposite, that is, not only anguished longing but also anhedonia or indifference.[14]

Raskolnikov experiences this double-edged *toska* throughout *Crime and Punishment*. Sonya also experiences anguish, yet hers is linked to her loved ones, while Raskolnikov's is largely objectless. In Epilogue, part 2, however, Raskolnikov's *toska* changes as Sonya becomes its object. This transformation not only signals his healing but reinforces the novel's message of love and faith—Raskolnikov the divided self, a young man who has privileged rationality over emotion and grace, finds wholeness by reconnecting to his moral emotions. On the novel's last page, Raskolnikov "could only feel. Instead of dialectics, there was life."

From the novel's outset, Dostoevsky's narrator not only identifies anguish as a source of Raskolnikov's physical and moral suffering, but also links it to Raskolnikov's first visit to the pawnbroker: "The feeling of endless revulsion, which had begun to oppress and torment his heart from the time he had first visited the old woman, had now attained such a dimension and was so clearly felt, that he did not know how to rid himself of his anguish" (part 1, chapter 1). Shortly thereafter, when Raskolnikov decides that his anguish derives from hunger and thirst, he felt "as though unexpectedly liberated from some terrible burden" (part 1, chapter 1). Although Dostoevsky will associate Raskolnikov's anguish with his shame, his theory of extraordinary men, and his decision to test his theory, he suggests that it began when Raskolnikov's mind

---

14 Nabokov characterizes *toska* as follows: "No single word in English renders all the shades of *toska*. At its deepest and most painful, it is a sensation of great spiritual anguish, often without any specific cause. At less morbid levels it is a dull ache of the soul, a longing with nothing to long for, a sick pining, a vague restlessness, mental throes, yearning. In particular cases it may be the desire for somebody or something specific, nostalgia, lovesickness. At the lowest level it grades into ennui, boredom, *skuka*." Vladimir Nabokov, commentary to *Eugene Onegin: A Novel in Verse*, by Alexander Pushkin, trans. Vladimir Nabokov, vol. 2, *Commentary and Index* (Princeton, NJ: Princeton University Press, 1981), 141.

starts to entertain thoughts that his conscience rejects. After reading his mother's letter, he feels that "all his present anguish, which had been engendered in him long ago, had grown, accumulated, and recently ripened and concentrated" (part 1, chapter 4). As a defense against his feelings of shame and guilt for being dependent on his mother and sister, he arrogantly elevates himself over others and repudiates moral principles on utilitarian and egoistic grounds, denying the equal value of all persons. After reading his mother's letter, Raskolnikov decides to seek relief from his anguish by committing murder, a decision that only intensifies his anguish and isolation.

Raskolnikov's anguish continues throughout the novel. After Luzhin leaves his room, "Raskolnikov, left alone, with impatience and anguish looked at Nastasya," willing her to leave (part 2, chapter 5). After he sees Afrosinyushka try to drown herself (part 2, chapter 6), Raskolnikov's anguish turns to apathy. After Dunya visits him at the end of part 5, Raskolnikov feels his anguish return (chapter 5). In part 6, Raskolnikov experiences authorial pride on seeing his article and then "a terrifying anguish gripped his heart" (chapter 7). On his way to confess, he is oppressed by an endless anguish (chapter 8) until he realizes that confession offers him a new possibility of wholeness. In short, from beginning to end of *Crime and Punishment*, Raskolnikov is weighed down by a feeling of spiritual anguish that dissipates only on the novel's final pages when he is resurrected in love.

Sonya's anguish, on the other hand, is intimately linked to her family, to her faith, and, as she reads the Gospel story of Lazarus, to Raskolnikov. On a micro-level, the Gospel-reading scene demonstrates how love for individuals is a sacred, even salvific, affair. Like Raskolnikov, Sonya is a divided self. Unlike Raskolnikov, who feels oppressed by his family's love, Sonya's love for her family sustains her and prevents her from committing suicide: "We're all one, we live as one" (part 4, chapter 4). She experiences anguish for her family and weeps for them. Finally, just as Sonya has sacrificed herself for her family, so, in reading the Lazarus story to Raskolnikov, she shares her soul and the strength of her faith with him. Sonya opens herself to Raskolnikov as she has opened herself to the Gospels.[15] In the climactic reading scene, she literally and figuratively shows him the way out of his self-enclosure by offering him new "air!" to breathe.

Raskolnikov and Sonya also share the spiritual and physical anguish (*toska*) of separation. Raskolnikov experiences anguish as an internal fragmentation brought about through utter pride, whereas Sonya experiences it through

---

15 Izmirlieva, "Hosting the Divine Logos."

utter innocence and humility. Raskolnikov focuses on himself, whereas Sonya attends to others. Raskolnikov's pride leads him to deny human interdependence. Even his fascination with failure and proclivity toward self-annihilation demonstrate his narcissism. Sonya, by contrast, intuitively acts as a moral agent who must stay alive to help those dependent on her. By creating contrasting portraits of anguish, Dostoevsky points to the larger thematic struggle between Romantic self-aggrandizement and Christian humility. Raskolnikov's ultimate conversion signals a rejection of abstract thought in favor of embodied love for another.[16] His decision to redeem Sonya's suffering with his "infinite love" represents a repudiation of isolation, an embrace of human community, and a return to God.

Anguish and love are only two of the moral emotions Dostoevsky employs to reinforce his novel's ethical and religious messages. In the Epilogue, he finally resolves the guilt-shame issue. In Epilogue, part 2, the narrator explains that Raskolnikov has fallen ill not from feelings of guilt but because "his pride was severely wounded; he fell ill from wounded pride." Such a categorical, iterated statement demands attention: readers must reconsider Raskolnikov's earlier illnesses. Like Nastasya, readers have made uncritical assumptions. While Nastasya assumes Raskolnikov's illness has an internal physical cause—"it's the blood" (part 2, chapter 2), readers assume it's the blood he has shed—his guilt. Yet in Epilogue, part 2, Dostoevsky's narrator confirms Porfiry's and Svidrigailov's earlier diagnosis—pride and shame lie at the root of Raskolnikov's suffering:

> Oh, how happy he would have been had he been able to condemn himself! He would have borne everything then, even the shame and disgrace. But he judged himself severely, and his hardened conscience found no especially terrible guilt in his past, except perhaps a simple *blunder*, which could happen to anyone. He was ashamed precisely because he, Raskolnikov, had perished so blindly, hopelessly, dumbly, and stupidly …

Raskolnikov suffers in Siberia precisely because he does *not* feel guilt. As the narrator observes, "he had not repented his crime." Readers infer that repentance would bring relief.

---

16 Workman, "Bone of My Bone."

RASKOLNIKOV'S SEMI-CONSCIOUS PLAGUE DREAMS

In addition to narratorial commentary, Dostoevsky employs scriptural short-hand to convey authorial message. After nine months in Siberia, Raskolnikov lies in the hospital haunted by semi-conscious plague dreams. The narrator calls them unconscious dreams (*sny*) but uses an impersonal construction indicating that they are "semi-conscious dreams" (*grezy*). Like the narrator's epilogic reporting, these dreams are more abstract, reflecting their cognitive nature: they express the enactment of great pride, individualism, and rationalism.

The plagues in his dreams originated in Asia and infected whole populations:

> Some kind of new trichinae appeared, microscopic creatures that settled into people's bodies. The people who had taken them into themselves immediately became possessed and mad. But never, never had people considered themselves so intelligent and unwavering in the truth as did those infected. Never had they considered themselves so unwavering in their judgments, their scientific conclusions, their moral convictions and beliefs. Whole populations, whole cities and peoples were infected and went mad. (Epilogue, part 2)

These trichinae dreams cause anxiety and discord, thereby reflecting Raskolnikov's emotional state: "All were anxious; they did not understand each other ... They did not know whom or how to judge, could not agree on what to consider evil, what good. They did not know whom to accuse, whom to vindicate. People killed one another in some kind of meaningless spite." Raskolnikov's trichinae dreams thus reveal his understanding that beings who lose their moral compass harm others—thereby resonating with his earlier dream of the mare. Whereas that first dream offered Raskolnikov the self-knowledge necessary to save himself (an impulse that gets derailed), these semi-conscious dreams, which occur after he has been in Siberia for nine months (a gestational period), and during Easter season, prepare readers for Raskolnikov's rebirth.

Dostoevsky intensifies the situational rhymes with the scene where Raskolnikov feels gripped by forces outside his control (Epilogue, part 2). After the dream of the mare, Raskolnikov experiences moral horror and resolves not to commit murder, yet once he hears that the pawnbroker will be alone the next evening, "he suddenly felt with his whole being that he no longer had any free-dom either of mind or of will, and that everything had suddenly and finally been decided" (part 1, chapter 5). In Epilogue, part 2, once Sonya joins him outside on the riverbank in the early morning, "how it happened he himself did not know, but suddenly something seemed to pick him up and throw him down at her feet." By evoking St. Paul's conversion on the road to Damascus, Dostoevsky hints at the presence of another dimension. Whereas in part 1, Raskolnikov returns to his coffin-like room feeling "like a man condemned to death," in the Epilogue's timeless landscape, he is resurrected "into a new life." More significantly, Raskolnikov has accepted Sonya's love.[17]

Near the end of his illness, Raskolnikov looks out his hospital window, sees Sonya, and steps away. The next day, he sees she is not there, realizes that he misses her, and writes to her. This step out of his self-enclosure allows Raskolnikov to leave the prison house of his shame and prepares him to accept and redeem his guilt. Raskolnikov has traveled a painful road from narcissism to self-sacrificing love: "he knew by what infinite love he would now redeem all her sufferings." Because Dostoevsky has identified Sonya so closely with Lizaveta, who is tied to the guilt script, Raskolnikov's acknowledgment of the suffering he has caused Sonya and his intention to redeem it demonstrate, on the novel's very last page, that Dostoevsky has finally given readers the guilt script we have been expecting all along.

Readers may object, as scholars continue to do, that Raskolnikov's resolve to make amends for how badly he treated Sonya does not equate to accepting responsibility for the murders. This can be answered by examining the links between Sonya and Lizaveta. The two friends are both meek, serve others, and believe in God. Sonya's Bible, which Raskolnikov asks for in Epilogue, part 2, is Lizaveta's; Sonya gives Raskolnikov her cross and wears Lizaveta's. Moreover, just before his shame dream of trying to kill Alyona Ivanovna again, Raskolnikov remembers Lizaveta—"Lizaveta! Sonya! Poor, meek ones, with meek eyes … They give everything … their gaze is meek and gentle … Sonya! Sonya! Gentle Sonya!" (part 3, chapter 6). When Raskolnikov confesses to Sonya with his eyes, she backs away from him just as Lizaveta had (part 5, chapter 4). When Raskolnikov takes responsibility for causing Sonya to suffer, many readers see this as the first step toward his accepting responsibility for the murder of Lizaveta, and eventually of Alyona Ivanovna. Maybe, maybe not, but

---

17 Caryl Emerson, "Bakhtin's Radiant Polyphonic Novel, Raskolnikov's Perverse Dialogic World," in *Dostoevsky's "Crime and Punishment": Philosophical Perspectives*, ed. Robert Guay (Oxford: Oxford University Press, 2019), 200.

considering the evidence, however subtle, allows us to see how tightly Dostoevsky constructed his novel.

As *Crime and Punishment* shows, Raskolnikov's moral emotions reveal his inner goodness. In the Epilogue, readers see more clearly that Raskolnikov's shame at his identity not only covers up his guilt at committing murder but proves he is not the extraordinary man he wants to be. He represses his shame and guilt feelings as they make him feel weak and passive. Once he realizes and admits his need for others and his duties toward them (which include accepting gifts, including love), he takes his first step toward Sonya, an opening of self. This internal shift effects an external shift—the hitherto hostile prisoners start to treat him more kindly. Finally, at the end of Epilogue, part 2, when he recognizes his love for Sonya, Raskolnikov can once again see himself as the moral agent that Dostoevsky's narrator, readers, and character-observers have been expecting all along. Love, the most powerful moral emotion of all, allows Raskolnikov to get past his shame, begin to accept his guilt, and rejoin the human community.

In plunging us into and taking us out of Raskolnikov's mind, Dostoevsky not only teaches readers to track his character's moral emotions and self-divisions, but also encourages us to see the costs of egoism, the benefits of altruism, and, most of all, the human need for interconnection. During the course of this great novel, Dostoevsky shows us what happens to a person who believes that rationality can repress and control the emotions. He fails. Denying, even trying to kill his emotions, causes more anguish. Only when Raskolnikov gives up control, literally flung, he knows not how, at Sonya's feet, can he find love, community, and salvation: "Love resurrected them; the heart of each held infinite sources of life for the heart of the other." Love, a positive moral emotion, thus prepares them for their next seven years of struggle—a period of biblical redemption. Sonya has a new family, and Raskolnikov has found a way to expiate his crime, even if indirectly. He may yet become the great man that his family, Porfiry, and Svidrigailov predicted he would become—but no longer in the egoistic, glory-seeking manner Raskolnikov had envisioned.

Discontent with the novel's Epilogue reveals that much of the novel's power comes from Dostoevsky's narrative strategy. Throughout the novel, Dostoevsky's third-person narrator stays very close to Raskolnikov, relating his conscious thoughts and unconscious dreams, describing his spontaneous actions and his rational afterthoughts. This closeness to Raskolnikov creates great sympathy among most readers for Dostoevsky's young axe-murderer. Even when Dostoevsky expands the novel's cast of characters, he largely employs them as doubles or foils that reflect other aspects of his protagonist. He thus keeps the focus on Raskolnikov even as he provides outside moral perspective on his thinking and its bloody outcome. By the time we get to part 6, most readers have moved from rooting for Raskolnikov's escape to favoring his surrender to the police. By providing others' views of Raskolnikov, the narrator gradually moves us out of Raskolnikov's divided psyche, until, like the novel's most perspicuous characters, we feel moral repulsion for the murders yet moral sympathy for the murderer.

The narrative strategy of the Epilogue thus surprises, even alienates, readers. The narrative summarizing in the first part of the Epilogue creates a psychological distance between readers and the novel's events. In Epilogue, part 2, however, the narration, albeit in very telescoped form, resumes its alternations between reporting Raskolnikov's thoughts and depicting his actions. Yet instead of reporting Raskolnikov's dreams as lived experience, the narrator summarizes them. Part 2 of the Epilogue thus recapitulates in miniature the move from the intense focus on Raskolnikov in the novel to the broader view in the Epilogue, part 1. Finally, part 2 of the Epilogue dramatizes Raskolnikov's resurrection from the outside, dips briefly into his thoughts, and then moves away again as the narrator ends his story. Through the novel and the Epilogue, careful readers feel Dostoevsky's authorial hand. Dostoevsky not only creates and controls the narrative voice, he sets the stage for the entire novel and its Epilogue.

Appendix 1:
Illustrations and Maps

Figure 1. Photograph of F. M. Dostoevsky by Mikhail Tulinov, Petersburg. 1861. Courtesy of Dostoevsky House-Museum, St. Petersburg

Figure 2. Haymarket Square in St. Petersburg. Lithograph from the drawing of A. Briullov. 1820s. Courtesy of Dostoevsky House-Museum, St. Petersburg

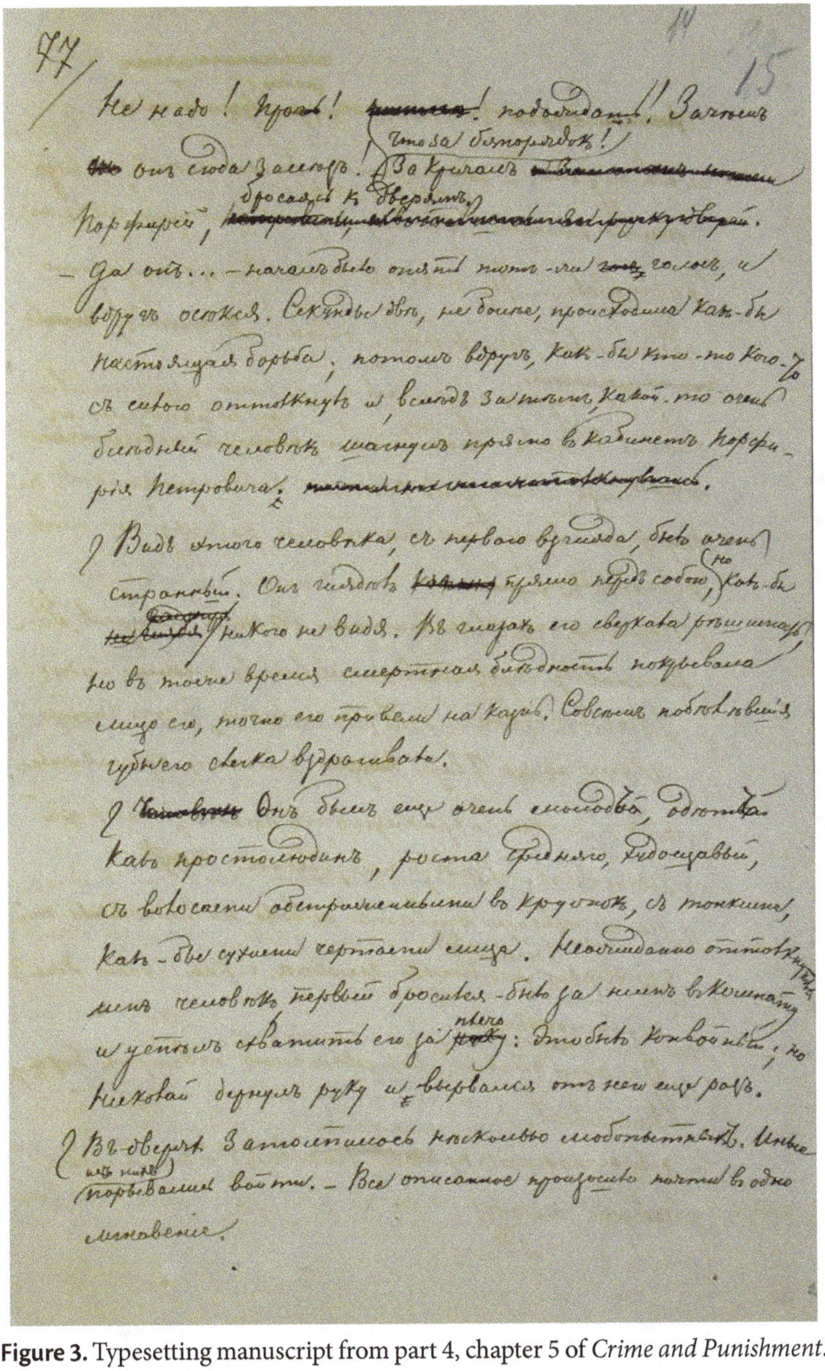
47

14 15

Не надо! Прочь! подождать! Зачемъ онъ сюда залезъ? Что за безпорядокъ! — Закричалъ Порфирій, бросаясь къ дверямъ.

— Да онъ... — началъ было оттуда чей-то голосъ, и вдругъ осекся. Секунды двѣ, не болѣе, происходила какъ-бы настоящая борьба; потомъ вдругъ, какъ-бы кто-то кого-то съ силою оттолкнулъ, и вслѣдъ за тѣмъ, какой-то очень блѣдный человѣкъ шагнулъ прямо въ кабинетъ Порфирія Петровича.

Видъ этого человѣка, съ перваго взгляда, былъ очень странный. Онъ глядѣлъ прямо передъ собою, но какъ-бы никого не видя. Въ глазахъ его сверкала рѣшимость, но въ тоже время смертная блѣдность покрывала лицо его, точно его привели на казнь. Совсѣмъ побѣлѣвшія губы его слегка вздрагивали.

Онъ былъ еще очень молодъ, одѣтъ какъ простолюдинъ, роста средняго, худощавый, съ волосами обстриженными въ кружокъ, съ тонкими, какъ-бы сухими чертами лица. Неожиданно оттолкнутый имъ человѣкъ первый бросился-было за нимъ въ комнату и успѣлъ схватить его за плечо: это былъ конвойный; но Миколай дернулъ руку и вырвался отъ него еще разъ.

Въ дверяхъ затолпилось нѣсколько любопытныхъ. Иные изъ нихъ порывались войти. — Все описанное произошло почти въ одно мгновеніе.

Figure 3. Typesetting manuscript from part 4, chapter 5 of *Crime and Punishment*. 1866. Courtesy of Dostoevsky House-Museum, St. Petersburg

Figure 4. Map of St. Petersburg. 1880. Courtesy of Dostoevsky House-Museum, St. Petersburg

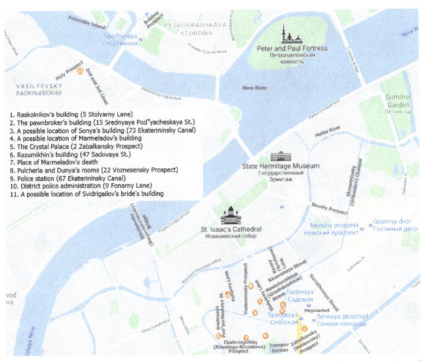

Figure 5. Early notebook page for *Crime and Punishment*. 1865. Courtesy of Dostoevsky House-Museum, St. Petersburg

1. Raskolnikov's building (5 Stolyarny Lane)
2. The pawnbroker's building (15 Srednyaya Pod"yacheskaya St.)
3. A possible location of Sonya's building (73 Ekaterininsky Canal)
4. A possible location of Marmeladov's building
5. The Crystal Palace (2 Zabalkansky Prospect)
6. Razumikhin's building (47 Sadovaya St.)
7. Place of Marmeladov's death
8. Pulcheria and Dunya's rooms (22 Voznesensky Prospect)
9. Police station (67 Ekaterininsky Canal)
10. District police administration (9 Fonarny Lane)
11. A possible location of Svidrigailov's bride's building

Figure 6. Contemporary map of St. Petersburg indicating some places mentioned in the novel. The putative identification of particular locations follows Vera Biron, *Peterburg Dostoevskogo* (Leningrad: Tovarishchestvo "Svecha," 1991)

Appendix 2:
Crime and Punishment Chronology

The main events of the novel unfold over two weeks, starting in early July—most likely, July 7, 1865. At the time of the murder, Raskolnikov (hereafter, RR) is twenty-three, Sonya is eighteen.

Day or date	Time	Events in the novel	Part and chapter
Day 1		early July, toward evening; a weekday	I.1
	sunset	RR's trial run	
		RR goes to tavern, where he meets Marmeladov	
	11 p.m.	Marmeladov's speech, RR takes him home	I.2
Day 2	after 9 a.m.	RR wakes	I.3
		RR receives his mother's letter and learns that the wedding is set for late July or mid-August	
		RR walks to Vasilievsky Island (via Voznesensky Prospect)	
		RR reacts to mother's letter	I.4
	1 p.m.	RR sees young girl on Konnogvardeisky Boulevard	
		RR falls asleep on Petrovsky Island > **dream of mare** (сон)	I.5
	9 p.m.	RR returns from Petrovsky through Haymarket, learns Alyona Ivanovna will be alone next day	
Day 3		Most likely, this day is **July 9, 1865**, the hottest day of that summer	I.6
	10 a.m.	Nastasya wakes RR	
	2 p.m.	Nastasya wakes him again and gives him soup	

Day or date	Time	Events in the novel	Part and chapter
		RR has semi-conscious dreams of oasis (грёзы)	
	6 p.m.	The clock strikes	
	7:10 p.m.	RR obtains axe	
	7:30 p.m.	RR arrives at the pawnbroker's	
	7:30–7:45p.m.	**RR murders the pawnbroker and her sister and gets away**	
		(Later we learn that at 7:45 p.m. Koch arrives; and by 8:00 p.m. the painters finish work)	
Day 4	2–3 a.m.	Drunks leaving tavern awake RR; RR cuts off fringe, etc., passes out	II.1
	after 10 a.m.	Nastasya wakes RR and gives him summons	
	after 11 a.m.	RR arrives at police station, signs document, hears discussion of murder, faints	
		RR buries evidence (plans to use canal, then Neva or Islands but buries it on Voznesensky near Isaakovsky Square)	II.2
		RR goes to Razumikhin's (via Konnogvardeisky > Nikolaevsky Bridge > Vasilievsky Island)	
		RR receives alms from mother and child and throws it (twenty kopecks) into the Neva	
	5 or 6 p.m.	**RR arrives home (after walking for about six hours)**	
		RR's auditory hallucination	
Day 5		RR is delirious for several days. This may be one of them. It is probably one of the four days he has had almost no food or drink—see note on Day 6	II.3
Day 6	10 a.m.	RR awakens (he has had almost no food or drink for four days)	
		RR receives money	
	6 p.m.	Razumikhin returns with clothes	
		Zosimov and Razumikhin talk about Mikolka and the murder, which happened three days earlier	II.4
		Luzhin arrives and learns that RR has been sick for five days and delirious for three days	II.5
	around 8 p.m.	As the sun is setting, RR goes out via Haymarket Square/Crystal Palace	II.6
		RR meets Zamyotov, the police clerk	

Day or date	Time	Events in the novel	Part and chapter
		RR witnesses woman's suicide attempt at canal and returns to scene of crime	II.7
		Marmeladov run over	
	by 10:05 p.m.	RR is on bridge over canal again; he goes to Razumikhin's, and then home, where he finds his mother and sister	
		meeting with family	III.1
Day 7	2 a.m.	Razumikhin reports to Pulcheria and Dunya (as related in III.3)	III.2
	7–8 a.m.	Razumikhin wakes	
	9 a.m.	Razumikhin visits Dunya and Pulcheria	
	around 10 a.m.	Together, they visit Raskolnikov and find Zosimov	
	12 p.m.	Zosimov leaves	
		Family visit continues	III.3
		Sonya visits; Razumikhin and RR go to Porfiry	III.4
		RR's first visit to Porfiry	III.5
		RR goes home; on the way he encounters the tradesman	III.6
		RR dreams of killing the old pawnbroker again (сон)	
	toward evening	Svidrigailov appears	
		Svidrigailov's visit	IV.1
	8 p.m.	Luzhin, RR, and Razumikhin go to Dunya and Pulcheria; Luzhin is thrown out	IV.2
		Family discussion; RR's silent confession to Razumikhin	IV.3
	11 p.m.	**RR's first visit to Sonya; at RR's request, Sonya reads the Gospel story of Lazarus. In total she reads twenty-seven verses: John 1:19–45.**	IV.4
Day 8	11 a.m.	**RR's second visit to Porfiry**	IV.5
		Mikolka's confession; tradesman apologizes	IV.6
Day 9		Luzhin and Lebezyatnikov; Luzhin gives Sonya 10 rubles for Katerina Ivanovna overtly and covertly slips 100 rubles into one of Sonya's pockets.	V.1
		Katerina Ivanovna's funeral meal for Marmeladov	V.2

Day or date	Time	Events in the novel	Part and chapter
		Luzhin accuses Sonya of theft; Lebezyatnikov exposes Luzhin; RR explains	V.3
		RR's second visit to Sonya, his "confession"	V.4
	sunset	RR goes home and finds Dunya there	V.5
		Katerina Ivanovna falls and coughs up blood; she is brought to Sonya's	
		Katerina Ivanovna dies	
		3 days pass	
Day 13		Before dawn, RR awakens on Krestovsky Island and goes home	VI.1
	2:00 p.m.	RR awakens late on day of Katerina Ivanovna's memorial service	
		Porfiry visits RR (their third encounter)	VI.2
		RR visits Svidrigailov in a tavern off Haymarket	VI.3
		RR and Svidrigailov talk in tavern	VI.4
		Dunya agrees to visit Svidrigailov	VI.5
	10 p.m	Svidrigailov visits Sonya	VI.6
	11:20 p.m.	Svidrigailov visits his young bride-to-be	
Day 14	12 a.m.	Svidrigailov goes to Hotel Adrianopolis (Petersburg District)	
Day 15	5 a.m.	Svidrigailov wakes from a nightmare and commits suicide before dawn	
	past 6 p.m.	After a night in the rain, RR goes to his mother's, then goes home, where he finds Dunya	VI.7
	sunset	**RR gives alms to a mother and her child**	VI.8
		RR's third visit to Sonya	
		RR at the crossroads; bows down and kisses the earth	
		RR confesses to Ilya Petrovich at the police station	
December 21, 1865 (five months after the murder)		RR is sentenced to eight years in Siberia	**Epilogue 1**
February 1866 (seven months after the murder)		Dunya and Razumikhin marry, plan to move to Siberia in five years	

Day or date	Time	Events in the novel	Part and chapter
April 1866 (nine months after the murder)		RR arrives in Siberia	
fourteen months after the murder (September 1866)		RR's mother, believing he will return after a nine-month absence, prepares for his arrival and dies two weeks later	
eighteen months after the murder (January 1867)		The Epilogue opens	
second week of Lent		RR is attacked for his "godlessness"	**Epilogue 2**
end of Lent through Easter (April 16) and Holy Week		**RR in hospital, where he has dreams (сны, ему грезилось)**	
second week after Holy Week		RR sees Sonya from hospital window, then Sonya falls ill	
after Sonya's recovery	6 a.m.	RR and Sonya are on the riverbank; RR experiences his "resurrection"	
seven years later		RR's projected release	

Appendix 3: Contemporary Critical Reactions

Dostoevsky studies are happily flourishing. The following works are among the most useful for reading *Crime and Punishment*.

DOSTOEVSKY AND THE 1860S

For Dostoevsky's biographical circumstances, the intellectual currents, and the historical background of *Crime and Punishment*, the go-to source is the fourth volume of **Joseph Frank**'s comprehensive biography (*Miraculous Years*, 1995) or the condensed chapters in the abridged one-volume edition (2010).

Many articles on the novel's historical and intellectual context can be found in the edited volume ***Dostoevsky in Context*** (edited by Deborah A. Martinsen and Olga Maiorova, 2015). For answers to frequently asked questions, see **Richard Wortman** on the Great Reforms and the new courts, **Barbara Engel** on the "woman question," women's work, and women's options, **Derek Offord** on nihilism and terrorism, **Jonathan Paine** on the economy and the print market, **Anne Lounsbery** on symbolic geography, **Konstantine Klioutchkine** on modern print culture, **Karin Beck** on foreign languages, **Ellen Chances** on Dostoevsky's journalism and fiction, and **Sarah Hudspith** on Dostoevsky's journalism of the 1860s.

DOSTOEVSKY'S POLEMICS

Liza Knapp (1996) argues that *Crime and Punishment* dramatizes the opposition between mechanical, deterministic laws of nature (seen in Svidrigailov's suicide) and religious resurrection in love (Sonya). **Harriet Murav** (1992) shows how the novel critiques and challenges the scientific psychology of its day by offering "the discourse of holy foolishness" as an alternative. **Greta Matzner-Gore** (2020) shows how Dostoevsky's rejection of the statistical worldview popular in 1860s Russia "influences everything from his methods of characterization, to the way he structures the novel's plots to the protagonist's improbable moral resurrection at the end." **Lynn Patyk** (2017) reads Raskolnikov as a proto-terrorist and examines his motives and actions in the context of nihilism and revolutionary terrorism. **Vadim Shkolnikov** (2021) views Raskolnikov as a "conscientious terrorist" and examines his actions in the context of rights and conscience. **Claudia Verhoeven** (2009) examines Karakozov's attempt to assassinate Alexander II. **Richard Peace**'s classic study (1971) outlines Dostoevsky's major polemics and thematics.

James P. Scanlan's philosophical study (2002) argues for Dostoevsky's philosophical sophistication and posits altruism and egoism as the poles of his moral thinking. His chapter on rational egoism is a must-read for the philosophically oriented.

For Russian readers, **Boris Tikhomirov**'s introductory essay and commentary on the novel (2005) are invaluable resources for understanding the novel's realia and intertextual dimensions.

NEW FIELDS OF STUDY

Amy D. Ronner (2010) views Porfiry Petrovich and Sonya as early practitioners of therapeutic justice. Both characters focus on Raskolnikov's need for confession, and both give voice and validation to Raskolnikov, urging him to take responsibility for his actions and confess of his own volition. In her latest book (2020), Ronner analyzes Svidrigailov's world as one of indifference, boredom, ghosts, and eavesdropping. Before and after he kills himself, Svidrigailov becomes larger than a single egoistic self-homicide: he is the reification of suicidal death itself.

Anna Berman (2015) treats *Crime and Punishment* as a family novel and looks at sibling bonds as a source of positive values. Focusing on the Raskolnikov-Dunya-Sonya relationship, she argues that the Dunya-Sonya vigil at the novel's end signals Raskolnikov's move from a consanguineal to a conjugal relationship. She also discusses the Marmeladov sibling bonds and Razumikhin as a brother figure.

Using trauma studies, **Yuri Corrigan** (2017) reads Raskolnikov as a "psychic fugitive," who spends his energies trying to forget and suppress "something" that oppresses and threatens to annihilate him from within. *Crime and Punishment* explores the various strategies that Raskolnikov employs to suppress that force—commitment to ideology, addiction to others or external stimuli, and extreme violence. According to Corrigan's reading, the murder temporarily protects Raskolnikov from the forces that threaten him from within until the novel's end, when they finally rise up and take hold of him.

Two excellent books treat *Crime and Punishment* **as a crime novel. Louise McReynolds** (2012) shows how the novel establishes a Russian preference for *whydunit* over *whodunit* crime novels, and **Claire Whitehead** (2018) shows how Porfiry Petrovich reflects and contributes to the widespread journalistic debates about the role of the judicial investigator. **Melissa Frazier** (2015) pairs Dostoevsky's novel with Wilkie Collins's *Woman in White* as a novel of sensation.

William Mills Todd III (2014) provides an overview of how serialization affected Dostoevsky's fiction.

LITERARY ANALYSES

Gary Rosenshield wrote the first and most comprehensive study of Dostoevsky's narrative strategy in *Crime and Punishment* (1978). In more recent work, he discusses the Pushkin texts with which Dostoevsky's novel engages, particularly "The Covetous Knight," which directly deals "with questions of power, crime, punishment, egoism, and ideology" (2013).

Robin Feuer Miller (2007) uses Dostoevsky's notebooks to argue that his move to third-person narration freed him from the obligation to provide a single motive. She also outlines multiple strategies for teaching *Crime and Punishment*, using her discussion of pedagogy to address broader questions of reading literature and reading generally. She uses Konstantin Mochulsky's paradigm—the novel as "a tragedy in five acts with a prologue and an epilogue"—as a hypothesis that encourages students to consider the novel's structure and the action of each part.

Robert L. Belknap's magisterial *Plots* (2016) argues that Dostoevsky's novel keeps multiple motives alive by challenging all causal systems. Belknap focuses on the novel's parallelisms and paradoxes, sees the collision between two theories of crime as an important plot mover, and reads the Epilogue as an ordeal novel (à la Bakhtin). Like Ksana Blank, he sees confession as part of the process of repentance.

Caryl Emerson (2019) draws on her knowledge of music to differentiate between the concepts of dialogue and polyphony in the novel. Dialogue belongs to the earthly realm and originates from individual voices which are unpredetermined and unstable, but always potentially tragic. Polyphony belongs to the eternal realm and is stable, true, hierarchical, and joyfully harmonious.

Ksana Blank (2010) explores Dostoevsky's idea that falling into sin may bring a person closer to God. She introduces the late sixteenth-century intertext of the "Tale of Andrew of Crete"—a great sinner turned saint who writes a famous penitential text—to reconsider the problematic issue of Raskolnikov's resurrection in the Epilogue.

Carol Apollonio investigates the disjunction between rumors about Svidrigailov and his actions in the novel (2009), noting that readers only hear of his evil actions yet only see his good works. More recently, she elaborates on how Dostoevsky develops epistemic uncertainty in his novels (2019).

Olga Meerson (1998) focuses on Raskolnikov's violation of the taboo on murder—both in thought and deed. She presents Raskolnikov's conflict with other characters as a collision of value systems represented by their personal taboos and argues that his moralizing voice finally triumphs over his rationalizing voice.

Malcolm V. Jones's first study (1976) offers a rich discussion of how the unintended and unforeseen consequences of the murder cause multiple forms of psychological, moral, aesthetic, and religious disorder, which affect all the novel's characters. In his second study (1990), Jones examines the way Raskolnikov's conflicting desires to relate to and to objectify others dramatizes his inner divisions and provides the grounds for his healing.

Robert L. Jackson's classic study (1966) identifies the two poles of Dostoevsky's aesthetics—*obraz* (form/icon) and *bezobrazie* (formlessness). His later book (1981) outlines the dialectic between compassion and contempt for humanity that drives Raskolnikov and moves him from hate/unfreedom in part 1 to love/freedom in the Epilogue.

The novelist **John Jones's** (1985) tour-de-force reading takes the novel's various threads, including repeated phrases, and weaves a stunning picture of Dostoevsky's narrative artistry and his ability to make readers live through its action.

Richard Rosenthal's psychoanalytic study (1984) shows how Dostoevsky inscribes psychic mechanisms into the novel, as in his use of projective identification and of physical space to represent mental space.

LAZARUS

While **Valentina Izmirlieva** (2016) sees Sonya's reading of the Gospel story of Lazarus as an example of radical Christian hospitality, **Eric Naiman** (2018) reads it as a Gospel rape. **Linda Ivanits** (2008) demonstrates how the understudied folk song about the rich and poor Lazarus (Luke 16:19–31) works with the resurrection of Lazarus (John 11:1–45) to fuse the novel's themes of resurrection and charity (gift for prayer). **Corrigan** (2017) holds that the story of Lazarus emphasizes "the concealed nature of the unconscious life, hidden, left for dead, and miraculously restored." **Berman** (2015) discusses Mary's and Martha's sibling love for their brother Lazarus. **Elizabeth Blake** (2006) argues that after her performative reading of the Gospel Sonya sheds the image of voluntary self-sacrificer (as seen by men) and voices a powerful Christian moral challenge to Raskolnikov's rationality. **Knapp** (1996) knits the Gospel reading into the novel's theme of resurrection through love, which overcomes the deterministic laws of nature. **Susanne Fusso** explains how the interference of Katkov, Dostoevsky's publisher, may have improved the Gospel reading scene (2017). **Ilya Kliger** (2018) recommends that students read the omitted verses—John 11:2–18.

THE EPILOGUE

Canadian Slavonic Papers has published a special issue—**62, no. 2 (2020)**—on the Epilogue, featuring four articles by Katherine Bowers, Kate Holland, Eric Naiman, and Robin Feuer Miller. **Bowers** argues that while the Epilogue logically follows the novel's events, it both fulfills and deviates from the generic plots informing it, a rupture that creates a sense of openness and possibility. **Holland** identifies the murder, the confession, and the conversion as three pivotal plot nodes, and re-examines the novel's temporal tension between deferral and anticipation of these three moments to explain the Epilogue's open-endedness as well as its connection to the novel. **Naiman** reads the scene closely and counterintuitively argues that the flatness of the Epilogue's tone inures us to the lurking possibilities that Sonya may continue as a prostitute in Siberia and that themes of incest and matricide still lurk. **Miller** reviews the three papers but adds her own view that the Epilogue is perhaps the most subtly dialogic and polyphonic text in Dostoevsky's fiction.

On a final note, **Michael Holquist** (1977) argues that the Epilogue takes on the time frame of the wisdom tale, which transcends the historical time of the novel's detective action. **Gary Rosenshield** argues that the narrative shift from indirect discourse to summary in the Epilogue permits Dostoevsky to convey authorial message and approval (1978).

TEACHING

In addition to Miller's 2007 discussion of pedagogy, see **Olga Meerson** on reading Raskolnikov's mother's letter (2014) and **Liza Knapp** on teaching Raskolnikov's dream (2014).

Look for the discussion about teaching *Crime and Punishment* on *The Bloggers Karamazov*, curated by **Katia Bowers**, and look out for a forthcoming MLA volume on approaches to teaching *Crime and Punishment*, edited by **Michael Katz** and **Alexander Burry**.

Appendix 4:
Chronology of
Dostoevsky's Life

1821	Born on October 30 in Moscow to Maria Fyodorovna, a merchant's daughter, and Mikhail Andreevich Dostoevsky, a doctor at the Mariinsky Hospital for the Poor, Moscow. The second of seven children, Fyodor grows up in a middle-class household run by his father, a former army surgeon and a strict family man.
1831	Dostoevsky's father purchases a small provincial estate in Tula, where young Fyodor spends four summers.
1833	Pushkin's *Eugene Onegin* is published.
1834–1837	Fyodor attends the Chermak Private Boarding School
1837	Dostoevsky's mother dies. He begins his training at the St. Petersburg Academy of Engineers, where he reads voraciously. Pushkin is killed in a duel.
1839	Dostoevsky's father dies. According to rumor, he is murdered on his estate by his own peasants.
1840	Lermontov's *A Hero of Our Time* is published.
1841	Dostoevsky completes the course at the Academy of Engineers; he is promoted to officer status and continues officer training but devotes himself to reading and writing.
1842	Gogol's *Dead Souls* is published.
1843	Dostoevsky begins service as a military engineer in Petersburg.
1844	Dostoevsky resigns from service to pursue literary career. He completes the translation of Balzac's 1833 novel *Eugénie Grandet* and begins work on his first novel, *Poor Folk*.
1846	*Poor Folk* is published. Dostoevsky wins friendship and acclaim of Russia's premier literary critic Vissarion Belinsky, author of the scathingly critical, banned "Letter to Gogol" (1847). Belinsky's approval wanes after *The Double* is published that same year. Dostoevsky meets the utopian socialist Mikhail Butashevich-Petrashevsky.
1847	"A Novel in Nine Letters" and "The Landlady" are published. Dostoevsky is diagnosed with and treated for epilepsy for the first time.

1848	"White Nights," "A Weak Heart," "A Christmas Party and a Wedding," and "An Honest Thief" are published. An almanac with Dostoevsky's "Polzunkov" is banned. *The Communist Manifesto* by Karl Marx and Friedrich Engels is published. Revolutions break out in France, Germany, Hungary, Italy, and Poland. Within the Petrashevsky circle, Dostoevsky joins a secret society led by Nikolai Speshnev, whose members plan to publish incendiary pamphlets.
1849	Dostoevsky writes *Netochka Nezvanova*. He is arrested for participating in the Petrashevsky circle and spends eight months in solitary confinement in the Peter and Paul Fortress. With several others, Dostoevsky is condemned to death and led to execution in Semyonovsky Square. Their sentences are commuted to penal servitude in Siberia, but mercy is announced only at the last moment, when they stand in their death shrouds awaiting execution.
1850	Dostoevsky begins his four-year internment at Omsk prison in western Siberia, an experience that will influence his later works. While imprisoned, he abandons the radical ideas of his youth and becomes more deeply religious; his only book in prison is the New Testament.
1853	The Crimean War breaks out.
1854	Dostoevsky begins four years of compulsory military service in Semipalatinsk, southwestern Siberia.
1855	Alexander II succeeds Nicholas I as tsar; his ascension is accompanied by some relaxation of state censorship.
1857	Dostoevsky marries the widow Maria Dmitrievna Isaeva. He publishes "The Little Hero," written in prison during the summer of 1849.
1858	Dostoevsky works on *The Village of Stepanchikovo and Its Inhabitants* and *Uncle's Dream*.
1859	Dostoevsky is allowed to return to Petersburg under police surveillance.
1861	With brother Mikhail, Dostoevsky establishes the journal *Vremya* (*Time*). *Time* serially publishes Dostoevsky's fictionalized prison memoir *Notes from the House of the Dead*, the novel *The Insulted and the Injured*, and numerous articles reflecting his native soil (*pochvennichestvo*) agenda. Emancipation of the serfs, February 19. Turgenev's *Fathers and Sons* is published.
1862	Dostoevsky travels to England, France, Germany, Italy, and Switzerland, a trip that inspires the anti-European outlook expressed in his *Winter Notes on Summer Impressions* (1863). While he is abroad, government censors order *Time* to halt publication, devastating his finances. Dostoevsky gambles heavily at resorts abroad, and often loses.
1863	Dostoevsky makes a second trip to Europe. He arranges to meet in Paris with Apollinaria Suslova, a writer whose story he had published the year before in *Time*. The two have an affair. In January, there is an uprising in the Kingdom of Poland (then part of the Russian empire). *Time* is banned for printing an ambiguous article about the uprising. The radical critic Nikolay Chernyshevsky publishes his utopian novel *What Is to Be Done?*, to which Dostoevsky will respond a year later in *Notes from Underground*.

1864	The Dostoevsky brothers establish the journal *Epokha* (*Epoch*), which publishes *Notes from Underground*. In April, Dostoevsky's wife Maria dies from tuberculosis. In July, Mikhail dies. First part of Tolstoy's *War and Peace* is published.
1865	*Epoch* collapses. Burdened with his own and Mikhail's debts, Dostoevsky goes on another failed gambling spree in Europe.
1866	*Crime and Punishment* starts serial publication in *The Russian Herald*, whose editor Mikhail Katkov also publishes *The Idiot*, *Demons*, and *The Brothers Karamazov*. Dostoevsky interrupts writing in October to work on *The Gambler*. He dictates *The Gambler* to a stenographer, Anna Grigorievna Snitkina, over the course of a month, and meets the contract deadline, thereby retaining rights to his published works, including *Crime and Punishment*. Dmitry Karakozov attempts to assassinate Tsar Alexander II.
1867	Dostoevsky marries Anna, who is twenty-five years his junior; the alliance is one of the most fortuitous events of his life. To avoid financial ruin, they live abroad for the next four years, in Geneva, Florence, and finally Dresden. Dostoevsky's epilepsy worsens. He begins work on *The Idiot*, in which the protagonist is an epileptic.
1868	*The Idiot* begins serial publication. Daughter Sonya is born in Geneva, but dies at only three months old.
1869	Daughter Lyubov is born. After reading about the murder of a student by the revolutionary Sergei Nechaev and his co-conspirators, Dostoevsky begins work on *Demons* and on a projected novel called *The Life of a Great Sinner*.
1870	*The Eternal Husband* is published. V. I. Lenin is born in the town of Simbirsk.
1871	Serialization of *Demons* begins. The Dostoevsky family returns to Petersburg, where their son Fyodor is born.
1873	Dostoevsky begins editing the conservative weekly *Grazhdanin* (*The Citizen*); his column "The Diary of a Writer" becomes a regular and popular feature.
1874	Dostoevsky resigns editorship of *The Citizen* and begins work on *The Adolescent*.
1875	*The Adolescent* is published serially in Nikolai Nekrasov's liberal journal, *Fatherland Notes*. In August, son Alexei is born. Police surveillance over Dostoevsky, begun in 1859, ends.
1876	Dostoevsky writes, edits, and publishes *The Diary of a Writer* as a monthly periodical. The January issue is 2,000 copies, with more printed in February. Six thousand copies of the February issue are printed. Dostoevsky buys house in Staraya Russa, future setting of *The Brothers Karamazov*. "The Meek One" is published in the November issue of the *Diary*.
1877	*The Diary of a Writer* circulation tops 7,000. In December, Dostoevsky breaks off work on the *Diary* to begin *The Brothers Karamazov*. "The Dream of a Ridiculous Man" is published in the April issue of the *Diary*.

1878	In May, Alexei (age three) dies suddenly. In mourning, Dostoevsky visits the Optina Pustyn monastery along with the philosopher Vladimir Solovyov to seek an audience with the elder Amvrosy, who becomes the prototype for Zosima in *The Brothers Karamazov*.
1879	Serialization of *The Brothers Karamazov* begins.
1880	In June, Dostoevsky delivers the celebrated speech on Pushkin at the dedication of the poet's memorial in Moscow. This is his last, triumphant public address.
1881	Dostoevsky dies from a lung hemorrhage on January 28 in Petersburg. He is buried in the cemetery of the Alexander Nevsky Monastery.
1912	Constance Garnett begins her translation of the works of Dostoevsky, introducing his writing to the English-reading world.

Bibliography

Anderson, Roger. "The Optics of Narration: Visual Composition in *Crime and Punishment*." In *Russian Narrative and Visual Art: Varieties of Seeing*, edited by Roger Anderson and Paul Debreczeny, 78–100. Gainesville: University of Florida Press, 1994.

Apollonio, Carol. *Dostoevsky's Secrets: Reading against the Grain*. Evanston, IL: Northwestern University Press, 2009.

———. "On Devils and Doors: Raskolnikov's Ontological Problem." *Dostoevsky and World Culture*, no. 1 (2019): 82–103.

Beck, Karin. "Foreign Languages." In *Dostoevsky in Context*, edited by Deborah A. Martinsen and Olga Maiorova, 258–63. Cambridge: Cambridge University Press, 2015.

Belknap, Robert L. *Plots*. Introduction by Robin Feuer Miller. New York: Columbia University Press, 2016.

———. "Survey of Russian Journals, 1840–1880." In *Literary Journals in Imperial Russia*, edited by Deborah A. Martinsen, 91–116. Cambridge: Cambridge University Press, 1997.

Berman, Anna. *Siblings in Tolstoy and Dostoevsky: The Path to Universal Brotherhood*. Evanston, IL: Northwestern University Press, 2015.

Blake, Elizabeth. "Sonya, Silent No More: A Response to the Woman Question in Dostoevsky's *Crime and Punishment*." *Slavic and East European Journal* 50, no. 2 (Summer 2006): 252–71.

Blank, Ksana. *Dostoevsky's Dialectics and the Problem of Sin*. Evanston, IL: Northwestern University Press, 2010.

Bowers, Katherine. "Plotting the Ending: Generic Expectation and the Uncanny Epilogue of *Crime and Punishment*." *Canadian Slavonic Papers* 62, no. 2 (2020): 95–108.

Chances, Ellen. "Dostoevsky's Journalism and Fiction." In *Dostoevsky in Context*, edited by Deborah A. Martinsen and Olga Maiorova, 272–79. Cambridge: Cambridge University Press, 2015.

Corrigan, Yuri. *Dostoevsky and the Riddle of the Self*. Evanston, IL: Northwestern University Press, 2017.

———. "Dostoevskii on Evil as Safe Haven and Anesthetic." *Slavic and East European Journal* 63, no. 2 (2019): 226–43.

Dal', Vladimir Ivanovich. *Tolkovyi slovar' zhivogo velikorusskogo iazyka*. 7th ed. 4 vols. Moscow: M. O. Vol'f, 1880–82. Reprint, Moscow: Russkii iazyk, 1978–80.

Dostoevskii, Fedor Mikhailovich. *Polnoe sobranie sochinenii v tridtsati tomakh*. 30 vols. Leningrad: Nauka, 1972–90.

Emerson, Caryl. "Bakhtin's Radiant Polyphonic Novel, Raskolnikov's Perverse Dialogic World." In *Dostoevsky's "Crime and Punishment": Philosophical Perspectives*, edited by Robert Guay, 173–207. Oxford: Oxford University Press, 2019.

Engel, Barbara. "The 'Woman Question,' Women's Work, and Women's Options." In *Dostoevsky in Context*, edited by Deborah A. Martinsen and Olga Maiorova, 58–65. Cambridge: Cambridge University Press, 2015.

Fanger, Donald. *Dostoevsky and Romantic Realism*. Chicago: University of Chicago Press, 1967.

———. "Apogee: *Crime and Punishment*." In *Fyodor Dostoevsky's "Crime and Punishment": A Casebook*, edited by Richard Peace, 17–35. Oxford: Oxford University Press, 2006.

Frank, Joseph. *Dostoevsky*. 5 vols.: 1, *The Seeds of Revolt*; 2, *The Years of Ordeal*; 3, *The Stir of Liberation*; 4, *The Miraculous Years*; 5, *The Mantle of the Prophet*. Princeton, NJ: Princeton University Press, 1976–2002.

———. *Dostoevsky: A Writer in His Time*. Princeton, NJ: Princeton University Press, 2010.

———. *Lectures on Dostoevsky*. Edited by Marina Brodskaya and Marguerite Frank. Princeton, NJ: Princeton University Press, 2020.

Frazier, Melissa. "The Science of Sensation: Dostoevsky, Wilkie Collins, and the Detective Novel." *Dostoevsky Studies* 19 (2015): 7–28.

Fusso, Susanne. *Editing Turgenev, Dostoevsky, and Tolstoy: Mikhail Katkov and the Great Russian Novel*. DeKalb: Northern Illinois University Press, 2017.

Holland, Kate. "The Clash of Deferral and Anticipation: *Crime and Punishment*'s Epilogue and the Difficulties of Narrative Closure." *Canadian Slavonic Papers* 62, no. 2 (2020): 109–22.

Holquist, Michael. *Dostoevsky and the Novel*. Evanston, IL: Northwestern University Press, 1977.

Hubbs, Joanna. *Mother Russia: The Feminine Myth in Russian Culture*. Bloomington: Indiana University Press, 1988.

Hudspith, Sarah. "Dostoevsky's Journalism in the 1860s." In *Dostoevsky in Context*, edited by Deborah A. Martinsen and Olga Maiorova, 280–87. Cambridge: Cambridge University Press, 2015.

Ivanits, Linda. *Dostoevsky and the Russian People*. Cambridge: Cambridge University Press, 2008.

Izmirlieva, Valentina. "Hosting the Divine Logos: Radical Hospitality and Dostoevsky's *Crime and Punishment*." In *The Routledge Companion to Literature and Religion*, edited by Mark Knight, 277–88. London: Routledge, 2016.

Jackson, Robert Louis. *Dostoevsky's Quest for Form: A Study of His Philosophy of Art*. New Haven, CT: Yale University Press, 1966.

———. *The Art of Dostoevsky: Deliriums and Nocturnes*. Princeton, NJ: Princeton University Press, 1981.

Jones, John. *Dostoevsky*. New York: Oxford University Press, 1985.

Jones, Malcolm V. *Dostoyevsky: The Novel of Discord*. New York: Harper & Row, 1976.

———. *Dostoyevsky after Bakhtin: Readings in Dostoyevsky's Fantastic Realism*. Cambridge: Cambridge University Press, 1990.

Karlsson, Gunnar, and Lennart Sjobert. "The Experience of Guilt and Shame: A Phenomenological-Psychological Study." *Human Studies* 32, no. 3 (September 2009): 335–55.

Kliger, Ilya. "Teaching *Crime and Punishment*." Lecture presented to the Literature Humanities faculty, Columbia University, New York, April 2018.

Klioutchkine, Konstantine. "The Rise of *Crime and Punishment* from the Air of the Media." *Slavic Review* 61, no. 1 (Spring 2002): 88–108.

———. "Modern Print Culture." In *Dostoevsky in Context*, edited by Deborah A. Martinsen and Olga Maiorova, 221–28. Cambridge: Cambridge University Press, 2015.

Knapp, Liza. *The Annihilation of Inertia: Dostoevsky and Metaphysics*. Evanston, IL: Northwestern University Press, 1996.

———. "Teaching Raskolnikov's Dream: Regarding the Pain of Others in the Classroom." In *Teaching Nineteenth-Century Russian Literature: Essays in Honor of Robert L. Belknap*, edited by Deborah Martinsen, Cathy Popkin, and Irina Reyfman, 82–96. Boston: Academic Studies Press, 2014.

Kostalevsky, Marina. *Dostoevsky and Soloviev: The Art of Integral Vision*. New Haven, CT: Yale University Press, 1997.

Lewis, Michael. *Shame: The Exposed Self*. New York: Free Press, 1992.

Lounsbery, Anne. "Symbolic Geography." In *Dostoevsky in Context*, edited by Deborah A. Martinsen and Olga Maiorova, 159–67. Cambridge: Cambridge University Press, 2015.

Martinsen, Deborah A. "Shame and Punishment." *Dostoevsky Studies* 5 (2001): 51–71.

———. *Surprised by Shame: Dostoevsky's Liars and Narrative Exposure*. Columbus: The Ohio State University Press, 2003.

———. "Getting Away with Murder: Teaching *Crime and Punishment*." In *Teaching Nineteenth-Century Russian Literature: Essays in Honor of Robert L. Belknap*, edited by Deborah Martinsen, Cathy Popkin, and Irina Reyfman, 162–74. Boston: Academic Studies Press, 2014.

Martinsen, Deborah A. and Olga Maiorova, eds. *Dostoevsky in Context*. Cambridge: Cambridge University Press, 2015.

Martinsen, Deborah, Cathy Popkin, and Irina Reyfman, eds. *Teaching Nineteenth-Century Russian Literature: Essays in Honor of Robert L. Belknap*. Boston: Academic Studies Press, 2014.

Matzner-Gore, Greta. "The Improbable Poetics of *Crime and Punishment*." In *Dostoevsky at 200: The Novel in Modernity*, edited by Kate Holland and Katherine Bowers, 159–76. Toronto: University of Toronto Press, 2020.

McReynolds, Louise. *Murder Most Russian: True Crime and Punishment in Late Imperial Russia*. Ithaca, NY: Cornell University Press, 2012.

Meerson, Olga. *Dostoevsky's Taboos*. Dresden: Dresden University Press, 1998.

———. "Theorizing vs. Teaching Literary Theory: What Is to Be Done with *Crime and Punishment*?" In *Teaching Nineteenth-Century Russian Literature: Essays in Honor of Robert L. Belknap*, edited by Deborah Martinsen, Cathy Popkin, and Irina Reyfman, 43–52. Boston: Academic Studies Press, 2014.

Miller, Robin Feuer. *Dostoevsky's Unfinished Journey*. New Haven, CT: Yale University Press, 2007.

———. "Afterword: In the End Is the Beginning." *Canadian Slavonic Papers* 62, no. 2 (2020): 144–53.

Mochulsky, Konstantin. *Dostoevsky: His Life and Work*. Translated, with an introduction, by Michael A. Minihan. Princeton, NJ: Princeton University Press, 1967.

Murav, Harriet. *Holy Foolishness: Dostoevsky's Novels and the Poetics of Cultural Critique*. Stanford, CA: Stanford University Press, 1992.

Nabokov, Vladimir. Commentary to *Eugene Onegin: A Novel in Verse*, by Alexander Pushkin. Translated by Vladimir Nabokov. Vol. 2, *Commentary and Index*. Princeton, NJ: Princeton University Press, 1981.

———. *Lectures on Russian Literature*. New York: Harcourt Brace Jovanovich, 1981.

Naiman, Eric. "Gospel Rape." *Dostoevsky Studies* 22 (2018): 11–40.

———. "'There Was Something Almost Crude about It All …'—Reading *Crime and Punishment*'s Epilogue Hard against the Grain." *Canadian Slavonic Papers* 62, no. 2 (2020): 123–43.

Offord, Derek. "*Crime and Punishment* and Contemporary Radical Thought." In *Fyodor Dostoevsky's "Crime and Punishment": A Casebook*, edited by Richard Peace, 119–47. Oxford: Oxford University Press, 2006.

———. "Nihilism and Terrorism." In *Dostoevsky in Context*, edited by Deborah A. Martinsen and Olga Maiorova, 48–55. Cambridge: Cambridge University Press, 2015.

Orwin, Donna. "Achilles in *Crime and Punishment*." In *Dostoevsky Beyond Dostoevsky: Science, Religion, Philosophy*, edited by Svetlana Evdokimova and Vladimir Golstein, 367–78. Boston: Academic Studies Press, 2016.

Paine, Jonathan. "The Economy and the Print Market." In *Dostoevsky in Context*, edited by Deborah A. Martinsen and Olga Maiorova, 66–73. Cambridge: Cambridge University Press, 2015.

Patyk, Lynn Ellen. *Written in Blood: Revolutionary Terrorism and Russian Literary Culture, 1861–1881*. Madison: University of Wisconsin Press, 2017.

Peace, Richard. *Dostoyevsky: An Examination of the Major Novels*. Cambridge: Cambridge University Press, 1971.

———, ed. *Fyodor Dostoevsky's "Crime and Punishment": A Casebook*. Oxford: Oxford University Press, 2006.

———. "Motive and Symbol." In *Fyodor Dostoevsky's "Crime and Punishment": A Casebook*, edited by Richard Peace, 75–101. Oxford: Oxford University Press, 2006.

Perlina, Nina. *Varieties of Poetic Utterance: Quotation in "The Brothers Karamazov."* Lanham, MD: University Press of America, 1985.

Rabinowitz, Peter. *Before Reading: Narrative Conventions and the Politics of Interpretation*. Ithaca, NY: Cornell University Press, 1987.

Robinson, Jenefer. *Deeper Than Reason: Emotion and Its Role in Literature, Music, and Art*. Oxford: Clarendon Press, 2005.

Ronner, Amy D. *Law, Literature, and Therapeutic Jurisprudence*. Durham, NC: Carolina Academic Press, 2010.

———. *Dostoevsky as Suicidologist: Self-Destruction and the Creative Process*. New York: Lexington Books, 2020.

Rosenshield, Gary. "*Crime and Punishment*": The Techniques of the Omniscient Author*. Lisse, Netherlands: Peter de Ridder Press, 1978.

———. *Challenging the Bard: Dostoevsky and Pushkin, A Study of Literary Relationship*. Madison: University of Wisconsin Press, 2013.

———. "*Crime and Punishment*, Napoleon, and the Great Man Theory." *Dostoevsky Studies* 23 (2020): 78–104.

Rosenthal, Richard J. "Raskolnikov's Transgression and the Confusion between Destructiveness and Creativity." In *Do I Dare Disturb the Universe?: A Memorial to Wilfred R. Bion*, edited by James Grotstein, 197–235. Beverly Hills, CA: Caesura Press, 1984.

———. "Gambling." In *Dostoevsky in Context*, edited by Deborah A. Martinsen and Olga Maiorova, 148–56. Cambridge: Cambridge University Press, 2015.

Scanlan, James P. *Dostoevsky the Thinker*. Ithaca, NY: Cornell University Press, 2002.

Shkolnikov, Vadim. "Dostoevskii and the Birth of the Conscientious Terrorist: From the Underground Man to Underground Russia." *The Slavonic and East European Review* 99, no. 1 (January 2021): 124–54.

Shohl, Margo. "Teaching *Crime and Punishment*, Step by Step." Lecture presented to the Literature Humanities faculty, Columbia University, New York, April 2013.

Tikhomirov, Boris. *"Lazar! Griadi von": Roman F. M. Dostoevskogo "Prestuplenie i nakazanie" v sovremennom prochtenii. Kniga-kommentarii.* St. Petersburg: Serebrianyi vek, 2005.

Todd, William Mills III. "'To be Continued': Dostoevsky's Evolving Poetics of Serialized Publication." *Dostoevsky Studies* 18 (2014): 23–33.

Verhoeven, Claudia. *The Odd Man Karakozov: Imperial Russia, Modernity, and the Birth of Terrorism.* Ithaca, NY: Cornell University Press, 2009.

Whitehead, Claire. *The Poetics of Early Russian Crime Fiction, 1860–1917: Deciphering Stories of Detection.* Cambridge: Modern Humanities Research Association, 2018.

Workman, Nancy. "Bone of My Bone, Flesh of My Flesh: Love in *Crime and Punishment.*" *Dostoevsky Studies* 18 (2014): 87–97.

Wortman, Richard. "The Great Reforms and the New Courts." In *Dostoevsky in Context,* edited by Deborah A. Martinsen and Olga Maiorova, 13–21. Cambridge: Cambridge University Press, 2015.

Young, Sarah J. "The Crystal Palace." In *Dostoevsky in Context,* edited by Deborah A. Martinsen and Olga Maiorova, 176–84. Cambridge: Cambridge University Press, 2015.

Index

Svidrigailov, 73–74; Sonya as double of, 41, 64; Svidrigailov's attraction to, 41, 47, 72

egoism, rational, 34, 100
Emerson, Caryl, 102
emotions, 15, 70, 79; of characters, 11; of narrator, 13; of Raskolnikov, 30; of readers, 10–11. *See also* moral emotions
Engel, Barbara, 99
Engels, Friedrich, 106
Epilogue, xii, 12, 97, 103–4; happy ending, 17, 78; new narrative strategy for, 78–81; as ordeal novel, 101; plague dreams, 82–85
Epoch [Epokha] (journal, 1864–65), 3, 5, 107
Eternal Husband, The (Dostoevsky, 1870), 107
Eugene Onegin (Pushkin, 1833), 105
Eugénie Grandet (Balzac, 1833), 105
evolutionary theory, 43
expiation, xii, 10, 19, 63
extraordinary man, theory of the, 11, 42–43, 66

farewell meetings, 68
Fatherland Notes (liberal journal), 5, 107
Fathers and Sons (Turgenev, 1862), 6, 106
feminism, xi, 6
first-person advantage, 10
Frank, Joseph, 99
Frazier, Melissa, 101
Fusso, Suzanne, 103

Gambler, The (Dostoevsky, 1866), 4
Garnett, Constance, 108
gender dynamics, 20
glasnost' (openness), 5
Gogol, Nikolai, 7–8, 105

"great man" concept, 35
guilt script, xii, 10, 17, 60; difference between guilt and shame, 63; readers' expectation of, 15; repentance and, 12

Hero of Our Time, A (Lermontov, 1840), 105
Holland, Kate, 103
Holquist, Michael, 103–4
"Honest Thief, An" (Dostoevsky, 1848), 106
Hudspith, Sarah, 99

ideology, xi, 5–6, 101; perils of, xii; psychology fused with, 17
Idiot, The (Dostoevsky, 1868), 2, 4, 107
Ilya Petrovich (Lieutenant Gunpowder), 31–32, 49, 77, 96
individualism, 82
inner monologue, 13
Insulted and the Injured, The (Dostoevsky, 1861), 106
investigatory literature, 56
Isaeva, Maria Dmitrievna (first wife of FD), 2–3, 106–107
Ivanits, Linda, 32, 103
Izmirlieva, Valentina, 103

Jackson, Robert L., 25, 102
Jones, John, 102
Jones, Malcolm V., 102

Karakozov, Dmitry, 100, 107
Katerina Ivanovna (wife of Marmeladov), 16, 19, 50, 66–67; boardinghouse daydream of, 65; death of, 65–67, 96; funeral dinner for Marmeladov, 56–57, 95; madness of, 64
Katkov, Mikhail, xi, 3–4, 103, 107